GROVE PRESS MODERN DRAMATISTS

Grove Press Modern Dramatists
Series Editors: *Bruce King* and *Adele King*

Published titles

Eugene Benson, *J. M. Synge*
Normand Berlin, *Eugene O'Neill*
Neil Carson, *Arthur Miller*
Ruby Cohn, *New American Dramatists, 1960–1980*
Bernard F. Dukore, *Harold Pinter*
Frances Gray, *John Arden*
Julian Hilton, *Georg Büchner*
Leonard C. Pronko, *Eugène Labiche and Georges Feydeau*
Theodore Shank, *American Alternative Theater*
Nick Worrall, *Nikolai Gogol and Ivan Turgenev*

Further titles in preparation

GROVE PRESS MODERN DRAMATISTS

J. M. Synge

Eugene Benson

Grove Press, Inc., New York

First published in 1982 by
THE MACMILLAN PRESS LTD.,
London and Basingstoke

First Evergreen Edition 1983
First Printing 1983
ISBN: 0–394–62432–7
Library of Congress Catalog Card Number: 82–82236

Printed in Hong Kong

GROVE PRESS INC.,
196 West Houston Street,
New York, N.Y. 10014

Contents

List of Plates

Plates 2(a), 2(b), 4(a), 4(b), 5(a), 5(b) and 6(b) are reproduced by courtesy of the Abbey Theatre, Dublin.

Acknowledgments

Grateful acknowledgment is made to Oxford University Press for permission to quote from *J. M. Synge: Collected Works*, and to the Macmillan Press Ltd for permission to quote from the work of W. B. Yeats.

E.B.

Abbreviations and Conventions

All quotations from Synge's published writings are taken from *J. M. Synge: Collected Works*, General Editor Robin Skelton, Volumes I–IV (Oxford University Press, 1962–8). References are included in the text and the following abbreviations have been used:

Poems	Vol. I, *Poems*, ed. Robin Skelton (1962).
Prose	Vol. II, *Prose*, ed. Alan Price (1966).
Plays I	Vol. III, *Plays*, Book 1, ed. Ann Saddlemyer (1968).
Plays II	Vol. IV. *Plays*, Book 2, ed. Ann Saddlemyer (1968).

Editors' Preface

The *Grove Press Modern Dramatists* is an international series of introductions to major and significant nineteenth- and twentieth-century dramatists, movements and new forms of drama in Europe, Great Britain, America and new nations such as Nigeria and Trinidad. Besides new studies of great and influential dramatists of the past, the series includes volumes on contemporary authors, recent trends in the theatre and on many dramatists, such as writers of farce, who have created theatre 'classics' while being neglected by literary criticism. The volumes in the series devoted to individual dramatists include a biography, a survey of the plays, and detailed analysis of the most significant plays, along with discussion, where relevant, of the political, social, historical and theatrical context. The authors of the volumes, who are involved with theatre as playwrights, directors, actors, teachers and critics, are concerned with the plays as theatre and discuss such matters as performance, character interpretation and staging, along with themes and contexts.

Editors' Preface

Grove Press Modern Dramatists are written for people interested in modern theatre who prefer concise, intelligent studies of drama and dramatists, without jargon and an excess of footnotes.

BRUCE KING
ADELE KING

TO
SIOBHAN MCKENNA
An Incomparable Pegeen Mike

1
A Brief Life

The City of Dublin has long been famous as a centre of culture; this was never more evident than in the second half of the nineteenth century when it was home to such writers of genius as Oscar Wilde, G.B. Shaw, W.B. Yeats, J.M. Synge and James Joyce. Of the five, it is Synge who grounds his dramatic art most exclusively in Ireland, finding in her legends and folk tales, and in her peasantry and their speech, the materials of such masterpieces as *Riders to the Sea, The Well of the Saints* and *The Playboy of the Western World.* He was, with Yeats and Lady Gregory, a director of the Abbey Theatre and it was his kind of theatre – rather than Yeats's – that was to influence the Abbey and shape a new generation of Irish dramatists. His is peasant or folk drama which manages, however, to sound themes that are of universal concern. In all his plays, he champions the imaginative life and condemns whatever seeks to restrain human liberty; he celebrates the richness of the solitary and the dispossessed (tramp and tinker) who are oppressed by society (priest

1

and mob); he dramatizes the plight of men and women whose existence in a menacing and meaningless world he invests with passion and poetry and brutality; he experiments with the form of the drama, wrenching it to new shapes to accommodate his uneasy fusing of the tragic and the comic. Synge's dramatic *oeuvre* is a narrow one, but it is central to the development of drama in the twentieth century.

John Millington Synge was born on 16 April 1871 in Rathfarnham, a suburb of Dublin. His father was a barrister and landowner, and a member of the Protestant Anglo-Irish class. He died in 1872 and Synge's formative years were powerfully influenced by his mother, a woman of strong and narrow Evangelical views. Her father, the Reverend Dr Traill, an Ulsterman, had been the rector in a Catholic village in the south of Ireland, and Synge's uncle, the Reverend Alexander Synge, had been a Protestant missionary to the Aran Islands, whose population was almost entirely Catholic. 'I have waged war against popery in its thousand forms of wickedness,' Traill once wrote from Cork, and Alexander Synge echoed him from the Aran Islands: 'I get on with the people so far very well, but how will it be when we begin to attack their bad ways, religion, *etc.,* I don't know.'[1] Synge's Aunt Jane used to lament loudly that she had not strangled the infant Charles Stewart Parnell when he had been brought from nearby Avondale to visit the Synges of Glanmore Castle, County Wicklow. Synge's spiritual and ideological journey from such an Ascendancy or Garrison background to the Gaelic-speaking, Roman Catholic peoples of Aran and Mayo and Kerry and Wicklow is one of the most remarkable in literary history.

Some of the circumstances shaping that journey can be traced in Synge's fragmentary Autobiography. His early schooling was continually interrupted by illness; without knowing anything of heredity he concluded that unhealthy parents would have unhealthy children and so resolved that he would never marry. Solitary by temperament, his sense of isolation was further heightened by his disillusionment with Christianity, caused in part by the severity of his religious upbringing.

> I was painfully timid, and while still young the idea of Hell took a fearful hold on me. One night I thought I was irretrievably damned and cried myself to sleep in vain yet terrified efforts to form a conception of eternal pain. In the morning I renewed my lamentations and my mother was sent for. She comforted me with the assurance that the Holy Ghost was convicting me of sin and thus preparing me for ultimate salvation.
>
> (*Prose,* p. 4)

When Synge was about fourteen he read Darwin, which reinforced his growing agnosticism and led him two years later to reject Christianity. 'This story is easily told,' Synge comments, 'but it was a terrible experience. By it I laid a chasm between my present and my past and between myself and my kindred and friends. Till I was twenty-three I never met or at least knew a man or woman who shared my opinions.'

Two famous Irish contemporaries of Synge also rejected Christianity in their youth. 'I was unlike others of my generation in one thing only,' W. B. Yeats recalled, 'I am very religious, and deprived by Huxley and Tyndall, whom I detested, of the simple-minded religion of my childhood, I had made a new religion, almost an infallible Church of poetic tradition.'[2] That poetic tradition he would find at its best in Ireland and things Irish. The other contemporary, James Joyce, was to have his *persona,* Stephen Dedalus, proclaim the necessity for the artist to fly not only beyond the net of religion, but also beyond the nets of nationality and language. Synge rejected Christianity and his Ascendancy class, and replaced them with a temperate nationalism and a deep interest in everything Irish.

Synge's rejection of his class was given impetus by the activities of his brother Edward, land-agent for the family estates in Wicklow and for various other estates throughout Ireland. The hatred in which such agents were held is best illustrated by Captain Boycott, Lord Erne's Mayo agent, who was 'boycotted' in 1880. (So effective was the boycott that Lord Erne's crops had to be harvested by fifty Ulster Orangemen under the protection of a thousand British soldiers.) In 1887 Edward evicted a tenant from his aunt's estate at Glanmore, County Wicklow, and demolished the wretched house. Although Synge does not seem ever to have written about his brother's activities (which were widely publicized), he did write about the evictions he saw on the Aran Islands ten years later. His moving account shows his deep sympathy for the evicted tenants, and the strength of his feeling may stem from revulsion at his brother's unsavoury activities. 'The outrage to a tomb in China', Synge wrote, 'probably gives no greater shock to the Chinese than the outrage to a hearth in Inishmaan gives to the people.'

There were, of course, wider and deeper causes that led Synge to embrace Nationalism. The death of Parnell in 1891 signalled a new phase in Ireland's fight for political independence. The nineteenth century had been a fruitful period of Irish parliamentary politics which had been dominated by two men of genius: Daniel O'Connell and Charles Stewart Parnell. In the 1880s, with Parnell's Irish

Party voting solidly as a block, no government in Westminster could function without his support. His price – Home Rule – seemed within reach. But the circumstances of Parnell's final two years – the revelation of his affair with Mrs Kitty O'Shea and the consequent divorce action – brought about his political downfall and contributed to his death. 'Do not throw me to the wolves,' Parnell pleaded, but members of his own party, aided and abetted by Gladstone's Low-Church constituents and the Irish Catholic bishops, deserted him. The Irish Party which Parnell had moulded into a single and powerful political force split into Parnellite and anti-Parnellite factions. The Christmas dinner scene in Joyce's *A Portrait of the Artist as a Young Man* dramatizes memorably this split within an Irish family.

The disillusionment caused by Parnell's death and its consequences caused the young generation of Irish intellectuals and writers to turn from politics to art. In this they were following in the tradition of the great Romantic poets – Blake, Coleridge, Wordsworth, Shelley – who dreamed of liberating mankind from the shackles that bound it; thus they had initially hailed the French Revolution. With the excesses of the Revolution, and the death of the idealism which had fuelled it, came the realization that perhaps the reform of political institutions did not necessarily bring about freedom. True freedom could only be achieved by poets who 'are the unacknowledged legislators of the world'. Blake's Prophetic Books and Shelley's *Prometheus Unbound* are the most important Romantic documents which stress the superiority of the liberation wrought by the imagination to that promised by political regeneration. In his essay, 'The Philosophy of Shelley's Poetry', Yeats writes: 'one soon comes to understand that his [Shelley's] liberty was so much more than the liberty of *Political Justice* that it was one with Intellectual Beauty, and that the regeneration he foresaw was so much more than the regeneration many political dreamers have foreseen.'

In their reaction to England and its colonial policies in Ireland the new generation of intellectuals and writers derided English culture and exalted all things Irish. George Moore dismissed the contemporary English theatre with the statement, 'Art is incompatible with Empire,' and Edward Martyn compared the 'vast cosmopolitanism and vulgarity' of England with the 'idealism founded upon the ancient genius' of Ireland.[3] The new writers, many of whom came from the Protestant Ascendancy class, dismissed English culture cavalierly:

> In the face of overwhelming material evidence of the superiority of one culture over another, the inferior culture elaborates a new myth in which it claims to possess the secret to a more holy, more moral, or more beautiful way of life. And most often in the case of this encounter of two cultures, the nativistic movement is led by a man who has learned the ways of the overlords.[4]

W. B. Yeats, a member of the Anglo-Irish Ascendancy, soon established himself by the force of his personality and the claims of his talents as the leader of the new Irish cultural movement. Indeed, the Irish Literary Renaissance may be said to date from the publication in 1889 of his first book of poems, *The Wanderings of Oisin and other Poems*. He was indefatigable in the promulgation of his artistic ideas and in founding literary societies, and he recruited the most able Irishmen and women of his time to help him in his work. 'I would have some of them leave that work of theirs [foreign scholarship] which will never lack hands, and begin to dig in Ireland the garden of the future, understanding that here in Ireland the spirit of man may be about to wed the soil of the world.'[5] This was written in 1901, but five years earlier Yeats had given Synge almost exactly the same counsel. The workers who gathered around Yeats were mainly of his own Ascendancy class and they constituted a brilliant group – Douglas Hyde, Lady Gregory, George Moore, A.E. (George W. Russell), John Eglinton, and Synge.

The cultural nationalism of the time led Synge, when he entered Trinity College, Dublin, in 1889, to study Gaelic. It was taught, under the aegis of the Divinity School, solely for the purpose of helping the Protestant missionaries to convert the Gaelic-speaking Catholics of the West of Ireland. If someone 'wished to learn a little of the Irish language', Synge recalled in 1902,

> and went to the professor appointed to teach it in Trinity College, he found an amiable old clergyman who made him read a crabbed version of the New Testament, and seemed to know nothing, or at least to care nothing, about the old literature of Ireland, or the fine folk-tales and folk-poetry of Munster and Connaught. (*Prose*, p. 384)

But Synge cared, and he read the Gaelic texts of *The Children of Lir,* and of *Diarmuid and Grania,* which was to influence him in the writing of his last play, *Deirdre of the Sorrows.* In Synge's final year at Trinity, 1892, Yeats founded the Irish Literary Society in Dublin. Although Synge was reading widely in Irish history and antiquities, he did not attend the inaugural meeting; ironically, he was spending the summer on the boycotted estate, Castle

Kevin, County Wicklow, and roaming the countryside noting down the stories of the tramps and the servant girls he met. He missed also Douglas Hyde's famous address to the new Society, 'The De-Anglicisation of Ireland', which led to the formation of the Gaelic League, dedicated to the cause of restoring the old Gaelic culture and the Gaelic language.

During the years Synge was studying languages at Trinity (he won prizes in Gaelic and Hebrew), he was also enrolled as a student at the Royal Irish Academy of Music where he received a scholarship in counterpoint and harmony. When he graduated from Trinity College he decided to become a professional musician and composer; he was encouraged in this by his mother's cousin, Mary Synge, a musician, who accompanied him to Germany and arranged for him to board with the von Eicken family who lived in a small town near Coblenz. The *pension* was run by four sisters, the youngest of whom, Valeska, became his special friend. To her he confided that he had recently fallen in love with Cherrie Matheson, the daughter of a strict member of the Plymouth Brethren. The anguish caused Synge by her refusal to marry him because of his atheism – or agnosticism – is reflected in his first play, *When the Moon Has Set,* begun in 1900.

Synge spent less than a year in Germany before he became convinced that he should give up music for a literary career. In January of 1895 he left Ireland to live in Paris hoping, like James Joyce a few years later, to make enough money giving English lessons to supplement his small allowance. His ambition was to become an interpreter of French thought and literature for the English-speaking world. For the next several years Synge lived in Paris studying literature and languages at the Sorbonne, reading widely in philosophy, ethics, socialism and politics (he attended lectures by Sebastian Fauré, the anarchist). He became interested in Breton culture, did some tutoring in English, and wrote poetry (mainly about his unrequited love for Cherrie Matheson).

During these years his interest in Irish culture and the Irish language deepened. He attended Professor H. d'Arbois deJubainville's lectures on Celtic civilization and later he reviewed *The Irish Mythological Cycle and Celtic Mythology* which had been translated by his friend, R. I. Best. In 1896 he met W. B. Yeats in Paris and it was on this occasion that Yeats advised Synge to go to the Aran Islands. Yeats also introduced him to Maud Gonne, the beautiful and fiery Nationalist who had fled to France to avoid arrest for aiding Irish tenants threatened with eviction from their holdings in Donegal. Under her influence, Synge, a member of the landlord class, joined the Irish League. Within a few months he resigned, feeling (correctly) that the League was militaristic in nature. Many years later, in 1907, he denounced the League because of its hostility towards *The Playboy of the Western World*: 'The Gaelic League is founded on a doctrine that is made up of ignorance, fraud and hypocrisy.'

In the autumn of 1897 Synge experienced the first signs of lymphatic sarcoma, or Hodgkin's Disease. A large glandular swelling formed on his neck and he lost most of his hair. He was operated on in Dublin; 'Under Ether' is a vivid account of his sensations while anesthetized. About this time he also began writing *Étude Morbide, or An Imaginary Portrait* which he later characterized as 'a morbid thing about a mad fiddler in Paris'. In 1898 he made the first of five visits to the Aran Islands which were to prove so important in shaping his vision and his art. After that first visit he alternated between living in Paris and Ireland and, apart from occasional reviews of contemporary French and Irish literature, he worked on *The Aran Islands,* an account based on his experiences during his first four visits to the islands. Yeats and Lady Gregory were delighted by it but were unimpressed by *When the Moon Has Set,* a turgid and melodramatic two-act play for which Synge showed a perverse predilection. 'The only thing interesting about it', Yeats wrote in a Memorandum to Synge's executors, 'is that it shows his preoccupation with the thought of death.'

The year 1902 was Synge's *annus mirabilis.* In that year he wrote *Riders to the Sea, The Shadow of the Glen,* and a one-act version of *The Tinker's Wedding.* In these plays he triumphantly discovered his métier and genius and marked out his literary terrain. Writers like John Masefield, Arthur Symons and G. K. Chesterton encouraged him by their praise, and Yeats and Lady Gregory drew him closer into their literary schemes. In March 1903 he returned to Paris to sell off his few belongings, for he had finally determined that he could work best in Ireland. Literary historians will delight in the irony that it was on this occasion that Synge met James Joyce, who had exiled himself from Ireland in the belief that he could best work on the Continent. Neither man liked the other. Joyce saw in Synge 'a dark tramper of a man and Synge saw in Joyce an ego with a mind that resembled Spinoza's.' Joyce sneered (pedantically) at what he termed the un-Aristotelian catastrophe of *Riders to the Sea,* but later paid it the compliment of translating it into Italian. When the English Players of Zurich presented the play in 1918, Joyce taught the actresses the *caoine* (Gaelic cry of sorrow for the dead), and Nora Joyce played the role of Cathleen.[6]

In 1903 Synge began work on *The Well of the Saints* and he made the first of four extended trips to Kerry. He discovered with delight the rich bilingual speech of the Kerry peasantry and the isolation of the Blasket Islands. *The Shadow of the Glen* was presented on 6 October 1903 at the Molesworth Hall. It aroused the anger of the Nationalists, most notably Arthur Griffith, editor of *The United Irishman,* who denounced the play as a libel on Irish womanhood. *Riders to the Sea* was presented in the same hall in February 1904, along with A. E.'s *Deirdre;* Synge's play as received without controversy, but with little general enthusiasm.

In 1904 Miss A. E. Horniman, an Englishwoman and an admirer of Yeats's work in the theatre, paid for the renovation of two adjoining buildings on Abbey Street and Marlborough Street and offered them rent-free to Yeats and the Irish National Theatre Society. The new theatre, the Abbey Theatre, opened on 27 December 1904 with a bill made up of two new plays, Yeats's *On Baile's Strand* and Lady Gregory's *Spreading the News,* and revivals of *Cathleen Ni Houlihan* and *The Shadow of the Glen.* The company had been recruited and trained by the Fay brothers. John Masefield, reviewing the opening night for the *Manchester Guardian,* wrote: 'they perform the best drama of our time in the method of a lovely ritual. . . . Their art is unlike any to be seen in England.'[7] Synge's *The Well of the Saints* opened to poor notices on 4 February 1905, although George Moore in a letter to *The Irish Times* praised Synge for having discovered 'great literature in barbarous idiom'. In 1905 Synge became a director of the Irish National Theatre Society and effective control of the Abbey Theatre passed into the hands of Yeats, Lady Gregory and Synge.

Synge's work was now attracting international attention. In 1904 *Riders to the Sea* and *The Shadow of the Glen* were performed by the Abbey company at the Royalty

Theatre, London, to good notices. *The Well of the Saints* was translated into German and performed at the Deutsches Theater Berlin, in January 1906. *The Shadow of the Glen* was translated into Bohemian and performed in Prague in the same year.

Synge – like Yeats – always preferred the company of women. He proposed marriage to Cherrie Matheson and to Margaret Hardon, an American girl whom he met in Paris, and was refused. In 1905 Maire (Molly) O'Neill joined the Abbey Theatre company and was given a walk-on part in the première of *The Well of the Saints*. In the January 1906 revival of *Riders to the Sea* she played the role of Cathleen and it was about this time that Synge fell in love with her. In the March 1906 revival of *The Shadow of the Glen* she took over the role of Nora Burke which had been created by Maire Nic Shiubhlaigh. Yeats remembered Molly and her sister, Sarah Allgood, as 'players of genius . . . one all simplicity, her mind shaped by folksong and folk-story; the other sophisticated, lyrical and subtle'.[8] When Synge came to write the magnificent love scenes of *The Playboy of the Western World* he had himself and Molly in mind, and he created the role for her of Pegeen Mike. His last play, *Deirdre of the Sorrows,* with its tragic insistence on the transitoriness of life and love, was conceived with Molly in mind as Deirdre.

When Synge met Molly Allgood she was nineteen, he thirty-five. Their relationship was a stormy one for Synge insisted that Molly 'play Galatea to his Pygmalion'.[9] Synge was intellectual and introspective; Molly was brilliant, flamboyant – 'so young and so quick and an actress' (Synge's description). Synge was highly educated, at the height of his artistic powers, a director of the Abbey Theatre; Molly was poorly educated, from the lower class, a Roman Catholic. Their relationship was not made easier by Synge's jealousy and his constant complaints about his health, which must have seemed like hypochondria – or morbidity – to Molly. In only his second letter to her Synge complains, 'it seems strange that you would not send me a line to tell me where you were'. Molly's response was to write *'Idiotic'* across the letter. But despite such outbursts Synge and Molly loved each other deeply; they became engaged and planned to marry.

Synge's most famous play, *The Playboy of the Western World,* was presented by the Abbey Theatre company on 26 January 1907 with Molly as Pegeen Mike, her sister Sarah as the Widow Quin, and Arthur Sinclair (later to be Molly's second husband) as Michael James Flaherty. Christy Mahon was played by the gifted W. G. Fay who had already created the roles of Bartley in *Riders to the Sea* and the Tramp in *The Shadow of the Glen.* The first two acts were received quietly enough but in the third act, according to Lady Gregory's account, the audience erupted in violence at the word 'shift'. Yeats graphically describes the disturbances:

On the second performance of *The Playboy of the Western World,* about forty men who sat in the middle of the pit succeeded in making the play entirely inaudible. Some of them brought in trumpets, and the noise began immediately on the rise of the curtain. . . . On the last night of the play there were, I believe, five hundred police keeping order in the theatre and in its neighbourhood.[10]

Synge wrote to Molly the morning after the première, 'I feel like old Maura today "It's four fine plays I have though it was a hard birth I had with every one of them and they coming to the world."' But his anger at the

13

hostility of the audience to *The Playboy* is evident in a letter he wrote to Stephen MacKenna: 'The scurrility and ignorance and treachery of some of the attacks upon me have rather disgusted me with the middle-class Irish Catholic.' When, however, the Abbey company toured England in June and presented *The Playboy* (censored for English audiences) at Oxford and London, it was praised enthusiastically.

But if Synge's literary prospects were improving, his health was deteriorating. The glands in his neck began to swell again and his doctor advised Synge to have them out. He did not know it but the swelling signified the dread recurrence of Hodgkin's Disease. Dr Oliver St John Gogarty, the Buck Mulligan of Joyce's *Ulysses,* advised him to have the glands out.[11] The operation took place on 14 September 1907 and when he was discharged he began making arrangements for his wedding. In October Synge felt well enough again to make another trip to work further on his Kerry book. But the coldness of his lodgings brought on his asthma and he returned to Wicklow where he seems to have begun work immediately on a play about Deirdre. 'I got a "Deirdre" fit yesterday,' he wrote to Molly on 22 October, 'and I wrote 10 pages of it in great spirits and joy.' Throughout the rest of the year he worked on the play, 'squirming and thrilling and quivering with the excitement of writing Deirdre'. In his last letter of 1907 to Molly he spoke of his writing, and his ill health. 'I have no fresh news since except that I'm hard at work as usual and that I'd pains in my inside last night. I think it's the cold.'

But it wasn't the cold; it was a tumour in Synge's side. He entered Elpis Nursing Home on 30 April 1908, and he must have sensed how serious his condition was. He wrote a letter to Molly the day before his operation with the instruction, 'to be sent in cover in case of death to Molly M. Allgood'. He also made arrangements to have his manuscripts entrusted to the care of Yeats and Lady Gregory. Exploratory surgery revealed that the tumour could not be removed. Synge was discharged from hospital on 6 July, but the doctors hid from him the fact that he was a dying man. The tone of an August letter to Molly is anguished. 'Next I am very unwell myself so I am going in tomorrow I think to see young Ball and have a talk with him. I cannot let things go on like this. I don't know what is going to become of me.'

Synge forced himself to return to his play on Deirdre while simultaneously preparing his poems for publication. Of one of these poems, written in September, Yeats said 'Magnificent'. Synge sent a copy of it to Molly on 10 October 1908:

I asked if I got sick and died, would you
With my black funeral go walking too,
If you'd stand close to hear them talk and pray
While I'm let down in that steep bank of clay.

And, No, you said, for if you saw a crew
Of living idiots, pressing round that new
Oak coffin – they alive, I dead beneath
That board, – you'd rave and rend them with your teeth.

(Poems, p. 64)

In October Synge travelled to Oberwerth to visit the von Eikens again and while he was there his mother died. He returned to Ireland on 7 November but although he continued to work on his poems and on his play he made little progress because of the increasing pains in his stomach. He entered the Elpis Nursing Home on 2 February 1909, still hoping to finish his play. On 23 March

Yeats wrote in his diary, 'Molly Allgood came to-day to ask where I would be to-morrow, as Synge wishes to send for me if strong enough. He wants "to make arrangements". He is dying. They have ceased to give him food.' The next day Yeats wrote, 'Synge is dead. In the early morning he said to the nurse, "It is no use fighting death any longer" and he turned over and died.'[12] Molly, true to her promise, did not attend the funeral.

In the months succeeding Synge's death, Yeats, Lady Gregory and Molly prepared an acting version of *Deirdre of the Sorrows*. It was presented at the Abbey Theatre on 13 January 1910, 'under the direction of Maire O'Neill', with Molly in the role of Deirdre. Yeats and Lady Gregory were in the audience and Yeats wrote how he 'was greatly moved by certain passages in the last act'. Certainly Deirdre's *caoine* over the slain Naisi is almost intolerable in its purity and tragic intensity:

> Let us throw down clay on my three comrades. Let us cover up Naisi along with Ainnle and Ardan, they that were the pride of Emain. [*Throwing in clay*] There is Naisi was the best of three, the choicest of the choice of many. It was a clean death was your share Naisi, and it is not I will quit your head when it's many a dark night among the snipe and clover that you and I were whispering together. It is not I will quit your head Naisi, when it's many a night we saw the stars among the clear trees of Glen da Ruadh, or the moon pausing on the edges of the hills.   (*Plays* II, p. 263)

We may pair this *caoine* with Yeat's moving lament written only a few days after Synge's death:

> Our Daimon is as dumb as was that of Socrates when

they brought in the hemlock; and if we speak among ourselves, it is of the thoughts that have no savour because we cannot hear his laughter, of the work more difficult because of the strength he has taken with him, of the astringent joy and hardness that was in all he did, and of his fame in the world.[13]

2
A Passage to the Aran Islands

I look on *The Aran Islands* as my first serious piece of work – it was written before any of my plays. In writing out the talk of the people and their stories in this book, and in a certain number of articles on the Wicklow peasantry which I have not yet collected, I learned to write the dialect and dialogue which I use in my plays. . . . *The Aran Islands* throws a good deal of light on my plays. (*Prose*, p. 47n)

Synge first visited the Aran Islands in 1898 and subsequently in the summer of the next four years. What he was to write of the Irish historian, Keating, might well have been applied to himself in 1898:

Apart from his natural talent he owes a good deal to his foreign studies . . . which gave him a knowledge of the outside prosperity of the world with which to compare the things he saw in Ireland, while in a purely intellectual sense the intercourse he must have had with men

18

who had been in touch with the first scholarship in Europe was of great use in correcting the narrowing influence of a simply Irish tradition.   (*Prose*, p. 361)

When Synge made his first visit to the Aran Islands he was a man of wide culture but he was not a writer; he lacked a theme and a style. 'The only way of expressing emotion in the form of art is by finding an "objective correlative,"' T. S. Eliot has written; the Aran Islands were to become Synge's 'objective correlative', furnishing him with both a theme and a style.

Yeat's meeting with Synge in Paris is one of those memorable encounters that evokes comparison with that between Coleridge and Wordsworth in the summer of 1797 which led to their collaboration on *Lyrical Ballads,* the central document of English Romantic poetry. 'Give up Paris,' Yeats told Synge. 'You will never create anything by reading Racine, and Arthur Symons will always be a better critic of French literature. Go to the Aran Islands. Live there as if you were one of the people themselves; express a life that has never found expression.' (*Plays* I, p. 63) It was good advice, for Synge at this period was very attracted to such writers as Pater, Wilde, Baudelaire, Mallarmé and Huysmans. A work of the period, *Vita Vecchia,* 1895–7, reveals how dangerous were such influences. *Vita Vecchia,* a suite of poems linked by a prose narrative, is a veiled account of his unrequited love for Cherrie Matheson. The sentiment is maudlin, the verse derivative, the syntax very often impenetrable:

> Five five this year my years
> Half life I live to dread,
> Yet judged by weight of tears
> Now were I calmed, were dead. (*Prose*, p. 22)

Another work of this period, *Étude Morbide,* illustrates the same pernicious influences. The diarist, a violinist, is in love with two women – his mistress, the Cellianini, and his new pupil, Mlle Chouska. They represent 'two parts of one ideal'. The contrast between the two women extends to another contrast between a life of asceticism and a life rooted in the senses. When the Cellianini goes mad and is taken to an asylum, the violinist contemplates suicide but is saved by reading her copy of the *Imitation of Christ.* 'I have never been so happy,' he writes. 'Beyond my readings of the saints and philosophers which I turn to three times a day, to suggest my will with power, I take some beautiful thing every morning and regard it till my admiration ends in a moment of passionate ecstasy.' But when he leaves Paris and lives for a time in Brittany, he finds that his interest in the saints and the Stoics begins to wane and is superseded by a more satisfying life of the senses. In a passage that anticipates the tone of *The Aran Islands,* the diarist records: 'Yesterday I was out fishing with some of the fishermen, and as I walked home to the village, sunburnt, hungry and healthy, with my old coat on my arm, I could not find any connection between my present self and the self of last winter's diary.' In the country he cannot think of Baudelaire or Huysmans 'without a shudder'. A late entry in the diary reveals clearly the genesis of many of the preoccupations that mark Synge's work: 'I am sick of the ascetic twaddle of the saints. I will not deny my masculine existence nor rise, if I can rise, by facile abnegation. I despise the hermit and the monk and pity only the adulterer and the drunkard. There is one world of souls and no flesh and no devil.' (*Prose*, p. 34) Among Synge's papers is an imaginary exchange between the author of the *Imitation,* Thomas à Kempis, and Rabelais in which Rabelais says, 'If I wasn't Rabelais I would be

Thomas à Kempis. The cool but passionate ecstasy. . . .'
The opposition represented here, and in *Étude Morbide*,
between saint and artist is continued in the opposition of
tinker–peasant and priest–saint in *The Tinker's Wedding*
and *The Well of the Saints*. Finally, the polarities represented in *Étude Morbide* by Paris and Brittany will be
represented again by Paris–Dublin and the Aran Islands
and, ultimately, by the materialism of modern society as
opposed to the imaginative world of the Irish tinker,
tramp and peasant.

Synge did not visit the Aran Islands for almost a year
and a half after his famous meeting with Yeats; but
because of that meeting Synge once again became interested in Celtic literature. He read Yeats's work – *The
Wanderings of Oisin, The Countess Kathleen and Various
Legends and Lyrics, The Land of Heart's Desire, The
Secret Rose* and *The Celtic Twilight*. In addition, he
studied the writings of the Breton folklorist, Anatole Le
Braz, whom he met at this time, and he resumed his study
of Celtic literature at the Sorbonne.

There are three slight pieces among the early writings
predating Synge's first visit to the Aran Islands which are
distinguished by their authenticity of tone and feeling, and
which suggest the artistic direction Synge was to take. The
first is a poem from *Vita Vecchia:*

> I curse my bearing, childhood, youth
> I curse the sea, sun, mountain, moon,
> I curse my learning, search for truth,
> I curse the dawning, night, and noon.
>
> Cold, joyless I will live, though clean,
> Nor, by my marriage, mould to earth

21

J. M. Synge

Young lives to see what I have seen,
To curse – as I have cursed – their birth.

(Prose, p. 19)

The power and bitterness of the poem may derive from
Synge's memories of his many childhood illnesses which
he associated with heredity. Certainly the poem has that
brutality of sentiment which Synge was later to demand of
poetry.

The other two pieces are 'On a Train to Paris' and
'Under Ether'. In the first of these Synge travels overnight
in a carriage with eight ballet girls. Moved by their youth
and vulnerability he asks: 'Is life a stage and all the men
and women merely players, or an arena where men and
women and children are captives to be torn with beasts
and gladiators who appear only to destroy and be destroyed?' When the girls wake up they ply Synge with
questions about Paris, 'throwing in at times a remark of
naive yet frank obscenity'. The gladiatorial image is
picked up in the concluding paragraph. 'Morituri te
salutamus! The pity I felt changed gradually to admiration
as I warmed myself with their high spirits and good
humour.' *(Prose,* p. 38) Here is the typical Synge note of
realism and morbidity: all are destined to die, but within
the tragic dimension of fate there is room for gaiety, even
obscenity.

The same sense of doom is expressed powerfully in
'Under Ether', an account of Synge's sensations when he
underwent an operation in 1897. 'I took notice of every
familiar occurrence as if it were something I had come
back to from a distant country. The impression was very
strong on me that I had died the preceding day and come
to life again, and this impression has never changed.'
(Prose, p. 43) Synge was a 'mortality-conscious and

22

time-haunted' man;[1] it was this profound sense of mortality which made him such an outsider. He was isolated from his family because of his atheism, he was isolated from the mainstream of Irish life because he was of the 'foreign' Ascendancy class, he was isolated from deep commitment to his fellow men and women because of his sense that human relationships were so fragile and so swiftly terminated. His sense of isolation found expression in characters like Nora Burke, Maurya, the Douls, and in Christy Mahon. Continually throughout *The Playboy* Christy craves marriage and a home; by the play's close he has come to learn that these are not for him. 'You're setting me now to think if it's a poor thing to be lonesome, it's worse maybe go mixing with the fools of earth.' (*Plays* II, p. 165) Synge signed his love letters to Molly with the signature 'Your Old Tramp', thus reflecting his relationship to the Tramp of *The Shadow of the Glen* (in which he had rehearsed Molly in her part).

An artist, especially one who has a deep feeling for natural scenery, must choose his terrain carefully. If he makes the right choice there will seem a proper inevitability linking writer and terrain like that between Wordsworth and the English Lake District or Thoreau and Walden. The same inevitability links Synge and the Aran Islands; those wild and desolate islands some thirty miles from Galway sparked in him an extraordinary form of nature-mysticism as profound as that of Wordsworth or Thoreau. In the Autobiography Synge records how the forces which rid him of 'theological mysticism' led him at an early age into certain 'psychical adventures':

> One evening when I was collecting on the brow of a long valley in County Wicklow wreaths of white mist began to rise from the narrow bogs beside the river.

Before it was quite dark I looked round the edge of the field and saw two immense luminous eyes looking at me from the base of the valley. I dropped my net and caught hold of a gate in front of me. Behind the eyes there rose a black sinister forehead. I was fascinated. For a moment the eyes seemed to consume my personality. . . . For many days afterwards I could not look on these fields even in daylight without terror.

(Prose, p. 10)

On the Aran Islands Synge experienced new modes of being in which physical and psychic perspectives were heightened – sometimes distorted – by the primitive character of Aran life and by the violence and starkness of nature. Nearly all biographical accounts of Synge stress his reserve and control, but *The Aran Islands* shows a feeling for nature that is carried almost 'to the pitch of a neurotic hyperaesthesis'.[2] The language and imagery is charged and intensely emotional – 'pitiable despair', 'passionate rage', 'wildest lamentation', 'terrible agony'. Following a magnificent description of a storm ('Then there was the bay full of green delirium . . .'), Synge writes: 'The suggestion from this world of inarticulate power was immense, and now at midnight, when the wind is abating, I am still trembling and flushed with exultation.' (*Prose,* p. 110) In another place he writes of the coming of night on Inishmaan: 'The sense of solitude was immense. I could not see or realise my own body, and I seemed to exist merely in my perception of the waves and of the crying birds, and of the smell of seaweed.' (*Prose,* pp. 129–30) The annihilation of the senses and the identification with consciousness described here may be compared with a similar experience described by the youthful Wordsworth. 'I communed with all I saw as something not

apart from, but inherent in, my own immaterial nature,'
he writes in a note on the famous 'Intimations' ode.

There are other points of comparison with Wordsworth.
In the Preface to the second edition of *Lyrical Ballads,*
1800, Wordsworth enunciated a startling new principle –
that in humble and rustic life 'the passions of men are
incorporated with the beautiful and permanent forms of
nature.' Synge, an admirer of Wordsworth, came to
believe this and incorporated the principle in his work. In
his Introduction to *The Aran Islands* Synge makes it quite
clear that this is not a guide book or a travel book. He tells
us almost nothing about the islands' history or antiquities
or churches; he is a diarist, a very selective diarist, who
reveals primarily the manner in which the Aran Islands
shaped his artistic sensibility and only secondarily the lives
and customs of the island people. *The Aran Islands* is as
autobiographical as *The Prelude* and might well have been
subtitled 'Growth of a Dramatist's Mind'.

The most obvious characteristic of that mind – and one
which has been much commented on – is its primitivism.
Hardly has Synge settled on Aranmore than he decides to
abandon it for Inishmaan where 'the life is perhaps the
most primitive that is left in Europe.' It is an extraordinary scene, this departure of Synge (as extraordinary as
Gauguin's abandoning of Paris for the South Pacific in
1890[3]), and we follow with astonishment his passage into
the primitive and the atavistic. 'It gave me a moment of
exquisite satisfaction to find myself moving away from
civilization in this rude canvas canoe of a model that has
served primitive races since men first went on the sea.'
(*Prose,* p. 57) His guide on this new island is a boy who
teaches Synge Gaelic and introduces him to the lives of
the islanders. Synge's spiritual journey is paralleled by
certain physical analogies. Within a few days he substi-

tutes Aran pampooties for shoes, and forces himself to learn 'the natural walk of man'. Continually he equates the primitive with perfection: 'The absence of the heavy boot of Europe has preserved to these people the agile walk of the wild animal, while the general simplicity of their lives has given them many other points of physical perfection.' In his enthusiasm for all things primitive, Synge even finds affinities between the peasant and the artist: 'The continual passing in this island between the misery of last night and the splendour of to-day, seems to create an affinity between the moods of these people and the moods of varying rapture and dismay that are frequent in artists, and in certain forms of alienation.' (*Prose,* p. 74)

Synge's admiration extends to the islanders' homes and their clothes. 'Every article on these islands has an almost personal character, which gives this simple life, where all art is unknown, something of the artistic beauty of mediaeval life.' Phrases like 'exquisite satisfaction' and 'beauty of mediaeval life' signal that Synge has not escaped entirely the artificiality of Pater and Huysmans, or William Morris's ideas on decorative art. Synge, especially in the first two parts of *The Aran Islands,* sometimes distorts the islanders and their lives precisely because he idealizes them.

But with each visit to the islands Synge sheds the subjectivity that marks very strongly the early experiences, in favour of a more scrupulous objectivity. In the first two parts of *The Aran Islands* Synge is often merely the rather subjective analyst of his own perceptions; gradually he learns to objectify what he sees. In the early parts he regrets his inability to relate more closely to the islanders. 'In some ways these men and women seem strangely far away from me. . . . On some days I feel this island is a perfect home and resting place: on other days I feel that I am a waif among the people.' There is no mention of this sense of isolation in Part Four, not because Synge had managed to bridge the difference between a highly cultured person like himself and these primitive people, but because he had come to realize that his primary business was to objectify their lives and their stories in his art. In Part One, for example, Synge listens to a story by the old *shanachie,* Pat Dirane, and records his reaction. 'It gave me a strange feeling of wonder to hear this illiterate native of a wet rock in the Atlantic telling a story that is so full of European associations.' In Part Four he meets two storytellers and his terse description of what happened reveals that he is now more interested in their stories than in his own reaction: 'We were at work for nearly six hours, and the more matter we got the more the old men seemed to remember.'

If the most obvious characteristic of *The Aran Islands* is Synge's primitivism, a second and complementary characteristic is his attraction to scenes of violence and death. An old woman is buried and, as the keeners mourn, 'thunder rumbled overhead and hailstones hissed among the bracken.' Synge goes out in a stormy sea and revels in the danger. 'Even, I thought, if we were dropped into the blue chasm of the waves, this death, with the fresh sea saltness in one's teeth, would be better than most deaths one is likely to meet.' Many of the stories he records are tales of death and violence. Ten men fight on the strand with knives 'and they never stopped till there were five of them dead.' A mother cradles the skull of her mother which has been unearthed while the grave is being dug for her drowned son. Like Hemingway who was also drawn to violence and death, Synge sees man as embattled and doomed in a hostile world.

This grief of the keen is no personal complaint for the death of one woman over eighty years, but seems to contain the whole passionate rage that lurks somewhere in every native of the island. In this cry of pain the inner consciousness of the people seems to lay itself bare for an instant, and to reveal the mood of beings who feel their isolation in the face of a universe that wars on them with winds and sea. They are usually silent, but in the presence of death all outward show of indifference or patience is forgotten, and they shriek with pitiable despair before the horror of the fate to which they all are doomed.   (*Prose,* p. 75)

We are reminded of Synge's encounter with the ballet girls on the train to Paris: 'Morituri te salutamus.'

One might question Synge's account of life and death on the Aran Islands on the grounds that he is, in fact, projecting his own obsessively tragic view of life on the islanders. Nowhere in his account does he show any feeling for the fervent Catholicism of the islanders which, presumably, might offer strength and solace in time of sorrow and death. Synge, rather, emphasizes their paganism. 'There was an irony in these words of atonement and Catholic belief spoken by voices that were still hoarse with the cries of pagan desperation.' Synge preferred a Greek and pagan *ananke,* for it allowed him to exploit and dramatize the starkness and despair of the human condition as he perceived it. Perhaps too, remembering his missionary grandfather's futile attempt to convert these people to Protestantism, Synge may have taken a certain mordant pleasure in making pagans of them.

Synge's account of the dangers encountered by the Aran fishermen is also a highly personal and characteristic one. In *Riders to the Sea* Maurya mourns the deaths of her husband, father-in-law and six sons, all drowned at sea. It will come as a surprise to most people to learn that in the course of the entire nineteenth century only twelve Aran islanders lost their lives at sea.[4] Synge himself records that when he was on the Great Blasket Island he was told that despite the dangers of the men's work there had been no one drowned on the island for forty years. But to reproach Synge for faulty statistics is like faulting Othello for not looking to his linen. The sea in both *The Aran Islands* and *Riders to the Sea* is a complex symbol of mortality and the point made by Synge in both works is that all men and women are riders destined to be drowned in that sea. Following the burial of the young man in Part Four Synge writes:

> As they talked to me and gave me a little poteen and a little bread when they thought I was hungry, I could not help feeling that I was talking with men who were under a judgement of death. I knew that every one of them would be drowned in the sea in a few years and battered naked on the rocks, or would die in his own cottage and be buried with another fearful scene in the graveyard I had come from. *(Prose, p. 162)*

Synge, like the Elizabethan dramatist, Webster, to whom he has been compared, was 'much possessed by death / And saw the skull beneath the skin'. His lack of feeling for the Catholicism of the islanders and his sensationalism, exemplified in the set pieces of the two burials which frame *The Aran Islands,* remain constant features of his work and receive their finest and most elemental expression in *The Playboy*. The early and idealized portrait of the Aran islanders is balanced by later detailed accounts of the islanders' cruelty to animals – 'They tie down donkey's

[sic] heads to their hoofs to keep them from straying, in a way that must cause horrible pain.' *(Prose,* p. 163)

Synge never lost his deep feeling and sympathy for the people of the Aran Islands or of the other remote regions of Ireland where he lived and travelled, but as he came to understand them better he modified the simple and Wordsworthian image of the peasant with which he began. In the preface to his *Poems* Synge wrote, 'It may almost be said that before verse can be human again it must learn to be brutal,' and it is this almost metaphysical conjunction of the ideal and the brutal which becomes Synge's characteristic note. There is a finely described incident in *The Aran Islands* where Synge exemplifies this conjunction. He is on a train travelling eastwards to celebrations in Dublin commemorating the death of Parnell. The train is full of soldiers' women 'cursing and blaspheming with extraordinary rage'. As Synge sits talking protectively with a reserved young girl, a sailor in the carriage 'talked all night with sometimes a touch of wit or brutality, and always with a wonderful fluency with wild temperament behind it.' Synge concludes: 'This presence at my side [the young girl] contrasted curiously with the brutality that shook the barrier behind us. The whole spirit of the west of Ireland, with its strange wildness and reserve, seemed moving in this single train to pay a last homage to the dead statesman of the east.' *(Prose,* p. 124) There is something curiously prophetic about this passage, as if Synge saw in this 'last homage' the sweeping away of his own deracinated Ascendancy class by the Catholic, Gaelic-speaking peasant class so alive and solidly rooted in poetry and brutality.

In his essay, 'Poetry and Drama', T. S. Eliot argues that Synge's plays form 'a special case, because they are based upon the idiom of a rural people whose speech is naturally poetic, both in imagery and in rhythm'.[5] This is largely true – and Synge himself has sanctioned this view. In *The Aran Islands* he has numerous comments on the beautiful intonation and diction of the people, the simplicity and attractiveness of the peasant talk, the art of the story tellers. And in the preface to *The Playboy* he stresses his debt to the folk-imagination and the language of the Irish peasantry. If we compare a passage from *The Aran Islands* with one from *Étude Morbide* (written in 1899 and partly revised in 1907) we can see plainly what Synge learned on the islands.

> The old man gave me his view of the use of fear. 'A man who is not afraid of the sea will soon be drownded,' he said, 'for he will be going out on a day he shouldn't. But we do be afraid of the sea, and we do only be drownded now and again.' (*Prose,* p. 117)

The immediacy of the observation, the vigour of the colloquialism, and the strength of the language, are in strong contrast to the following paragraph:

> I have seen symphonies of colour that moved with musical recurrence round centres I could not understand: I have passed the solitude of seas and felt with cold hands the tropical profusion in their caverns of undulating gloom and then all these things rolled themselves in a vortex and left a single lily in their wake.
> (*Prose,* p. 34)

And yet, while we can make full allowance for Synge's belief that all art is a collaboration, we must not underestimate his genius in modifying and adapting the language and idioms and stories which he heard:

Where in prose drama language tends to be transparent, allowing us direct access to the meaning of the speaker, or by small distortions suggesting his character, in poetry meaning is expressed through the very colour and tone of the medium itself. It is in this sense, ultimately, that Synge's language is poetic and his own creation.[6]

The importance of Synge's experiences on the Aran Islands cannot be overestimated; here he found the plots of three of his plays, and innumerable incidents, images, and turns of speech that provided the raw data on which his creative imagination could work. These he had been unable to find in Europe or in contemporary European literature. James Joyce was especially troubled by the thought that Synge in choosing to return to Ireland had proved him, the Continentalist, wrong. When he read of the rows that followed the presentation of *The Playboy* he told his brother that 'the news put me off the story I was going to write – to wit, *The Dead.*'[7] When he finally did write the story, parallels between his life and Synge's may well have influenced its shaping. In 'The Dead' Gabriel Conroy is a reviewer for the *Daily Express* (as were both Synge and Joyce), he spends his vacations on the Continent but is urged by the Gaelic-speaking Miss Ivors to go to the Aran Islands: '"And haven't you your own land to visit," continued Miss Ivors, "that you know nothing of, your own people, and your own country?"'[8] The story suggests that Conroy is an ineffectual artist and lover because he has denied his roots and become a West Briton, a traitor to his class. Later he discovers that his wife who comes from the West of Ireland (like Nora, Joyce's wife) still loves Michael Furey of Galway. Furey is clearly associated with a Gaelic culture. At the story's close Conroy has come to see the futility of his life and he resolves that he too must make a journey to the West of Ireland. 'The time had come for him to set out on his journey westwards.' While the conclusion of 'The Dead' is richly ambiguous about the outcome of this journey, there is nothing ambiguous about the outcome of Synge's passage to the Aran Islands. Yeats catches wonderfully the inevitability that links Synge's genius and the Aran Islands:

> long travelling, he had come
> Towards nightfall among certain set apart
> In a most desolate stony place,
> Towards nightfall upon a race
> Passionate and simple like his heart.[9]

3
Synge and the Theatre

'Where, but for that conversation at Florimond de Basterot's,' Yeats wondered, 'had been the genius of Synge?'[1] The conversation referred to took place in July 1897 when he, Lady Gregory and Edward Martyn discussed the feasibility of founding an Irish theatre. The upshot was that a letter was prepared soliciting support and funds, and setting out the ideals of the trio:

We propose to have performed in Dublin, in the spring of every year certain Celtic and Irish plays, which whatever be their degree of excellence will be written with a high ambition, and so build up a Celtic and Irish school of dramatic literature. We hope to find in Ireland an uncorrupted and imaginative audience trained to listen by its passion for oratory, and believe that our desire to bring upon the stage the deeper thoughts and emotions of Ireland will ensure for us a tolerant welcome, and that freedom to experiment which is not found in theatres of England, and without which no new movement in art or literature can succeed. We will show that Ireland is not the home of buffoonery and of easy sentiment, as it has been represented, but the home of an ancient idealism. We are confident of the support of all Irish people who are weary of misrepresentation, in carrying out a work that is outside all the political questions that divide us.[2]

When enough money was guaranteed to finance the new Irish Literary Theatre, it was decided to take a Dublin theatre and present Martyn's *Heather Field* and Yeats's *The Countess Cathleen*. But since the founders proposed a three-year period of experiment it was imperative to find playwrights who would help develop this new 'Celtic and Irish school of dramatic literature'. It may have been with an eye to that imperative that Yeats wrote to Synge on 23 June 1898 inviting him to stop off on his way from the Aran Islands at Coole Park, the home of Lady Gregory, to 'talk about Aran and your work there'.[3] One suspects that the talk turned less on Synge's work than on Yeats's plans for the new Irish Theatre. Neither Synge nor Lady Gregory had yet published anything whereas Yeats had already established a reputation as poet, essayist, folklorist, editor and dramatist. One of his plays, *The Land of Heart's Desire,* had been performed in London in 1894 on a double bill with G. B. Shaw's *Arms and the Man.*

From the beginning of his career as a dramatist Yeats was remarkably clear as to the kind of drama he wanted. Certainly his practice was modified as he learned the dramatist's craft and as his vision deepened and expanded, but there are certain basic artistic assumptions underlying his practice which remain constant. The most important of these assumptions, which he expressed as early as 1899, emphasizes the primacy of the imagination in drama. Lack of imagination explains the impoverishment of the contemporary stage. In a letter of 27 January 1899 to the editor of the *Daily Chronicle* Yeats wrote:

> The accepted theory is that men of letters suddenly lost the dramatic faculty, but it is easier to believe that times and seasons change than that the imagination and intellect change: for imagination and intellect are that which is eternal in man crying out against that which is temporal and perishing.[4]

In the same letter Yeats calls for 'scenery and costumes which will draw little attention to themselves and cost little money', and for a theatre where preference is given to the spoken word rather than to visual effects.

Four years later, in 'The Reform of the Theatre', Yeats elaborates on these ideas and announces four principles which should govern the activities of the Irish Literary Theatre:

> *First.* We have to write or find plays that will make the theatre a place of intellectual excitement – a place where the mind goes to be liberated as it was liberated by the theatres of Greece and England and France at certain great moments of their history, and as it is liberated in Scandinavia to-day. . . .
> *Second.* But if we are to restore words to their sovereignty we must make speech even more important than gesture upon the stage. . . .
> *Third.* We must simplify acting, especially in poetical drama, and in prose drama that is remote from real life like my *Hour-Glass*. . . .
> *Fourth.* Just as it is necessary to simplify gesture that it

may accompany speech without being its rival, it is necessary to simplify both the form and colour of scenery and costume.[5]

The reference to Scandinavia shows Yeats's awareness of the work of Ibsen and Björnson, which he held to be rooted in the old Scandinavian epic literature and in the literature of the modern peasant. Yeats applied the same ideas to Ireland believing that it was on the verge of a literary renaissance in which the rich imagination and speech of the people could be tapped. 'We have turned a great deal of Irish imagination towards the stage,' he wrote in 1901.

We could not have done this if our movement had not opened a way of expression for an impulse that was in the people themselves. The truth is that the Irish people are at that precise stage of their history when imagination, shaped by many stirring events, desires dramatic expression.[6]

In another essay, Yeats spoke of the kind of play he wanted written and performed:

. . . plays about the life and artisans and countrypeople are the best worth getting. In time, I think, we can make the poetical play a living dramatic form again, and the training our actors will get from plays of country life, with its unchanging outline, its abundant speech, its extravagance of thought, will help to establish a school of imaginative acting.[7]

There is much in these ideas with which Synge would have been in complete agreement. Like Yeats Synge makes continual reference to the role of the imagination. In the preface to *The Tinker's Wedding* he writes: 'The drama is made serious – in the French sense of the word – not by the degree in which it is taken up with problems that are serious in themselves, but by the degree in which it gives the nourishment, not very easy to define, on which our imaginations live.' Like Yeats he emphasizes the literary character of the Irish dramatic movement. 'The whole interest of our movement is that our little plays try to be literature first – i.e. to be personal, sincere, and beautiful – and drama afterwards.' (*Plays* I, p. xxvii) In the preface to *The Playboy of the Western World* he links imagination and language as Yeats does:

> In countries where the imagination of the people, and the language they use, is rich and living, it is possible for a writer to be rich and copious in his words, and at the same time to give the reality which is the root of all poetry, in a comprehensive and natural form.

In the same preface Synge argues that modern European literature is unable to offer the contemporary dramatist a model because it is a 'literature of towns'. Mallarmé and Huysmans are decadent writers who produce books unrelated to 'the profound and common interests of life'; Ibsen and Zola may concern themselves with life but they do so in 'joyless and pallid words'. Synge, like Yeats, is insistent that the reality of life can only be expressed in the living idiom of an everyday speech; he further argues that on the stage 'one must have reality, and one must have joy.'

The term 'joy' is a complex one. Synge clearly associates it with the vitality of the imagination in somewhat the same manner as Coleridge in the famous 'Dejection: An Ode':

> Joy is the sweet voice, Joy the luminous cloud –
> > We in ourselves rejoice!
> And thence flows all that charms or ear or sight,
> > All melodies the echoes of that voice,
> All colours a suffusion from that light.

In his essay, 'J. M. Synge and the Ireland of his Time', Yeats too provides a perceptive gloss on the term.

> There is in the creative joy an acceptance of what life brings, because we have understood the beauty of what it brings, or a hatred of death for what it takes away, which arouses within us, through some sympathy perhaps with all other men, an energy so noble, so powerful, that we laugh aloud and mock, in the terror or the sweetness of our exaltation, at death and oblivion.[8]

Like Yeats, Synge believed that there could still be found in Ireland that poetic imagination and a living language from which true drama could be created:

> In a good play every speech should be as fully flavoured as a nut or apple, and such speeches cannot be written by any one who works among people who have shut their lips on poetry. In Ireland, for a few years more, we have a popular imagination that is fiery, and magnificent, and tender. *(Plays* II, p.45)

But if Synge and Yeats shared a number of artistic principles, they differed greatly in their practice. 'All that we did, all that we said or sang / Must come from contact with the soil,' Yeats wrote,[9] but he very soon deserted the soil for the drawing-room. Even before he became interested in the Japanese Noh play there is evidence that he favoured a 'pure' drama where character and incident were less important than mood and symbol. He makes the point as early as 1899 when describing his play, *The Countess Cathleen*: 'The play is not historic, but symbolic, and has as little to do with any definite place and time as an *auto* by Calderon.'[10] He de-emphasized character in order to highlight the heroic and the ritualistic, and gradually the mask and the dance threatened to supplant the actor. By 1916 Yeats, now experimenting enthusiastically with the stylized conventions of Noh drama, wrote: 'I have invented a form of drama, distinguished, indirect, and symbolic, and having no need of mob or Press to pay its way – an aristocratic form.'[11] He had finally moved from the soil of Ireland to the London drawing-room of Lady Cunard.

Synge, on the other hand, grounds his drama firmly in character and incident. Perhaps he had Yeats in mind when he wrote in the preface to his *Poems,* 'The poetry of exaltation will be always the highest, but when men lose their poetic feeling for ordinary life, and cannot write poetry of ordinary things, their exalted poetry is likely to lose its strength of exaltation.' Ordinary life, ordinary things. It was this quality that Yeats lacked. But it was there in the poetry of Villon and Herrick and Burns, as Synge pointed out in the same preface. Again, he may have been thinking of Yeats's work when he claims that the poetry of these men was read by 'strong men, and thieves, and deacons, not by little cliques only'. Synge had little liking or affinity for the melancholy spirituality of the Celtic Twilight or the artificiality of *fin de siècle* poets. The timber of poetry, he argues in a striking phrase, must have 'strong roots among the clay and worms'. If Synge's interest in the clay and worms, portrayed so graphically in poems like 'Danny' or 'A Question', or in the final scene of *The Playboy* where Christy Mahon is tortured, seems brutal, that brutality was deliberately sought. 'It may almost be said that before verse can be human again it must learn to be brutal,' he declared.

> Then Danny smashed the nose on Byrne,
> He split the lips on three,
> And bit across the right hand thumb
> Of one Red Shawn Magee.

(Poems, p. 56)

The 'brutal' embraces more than the physically brutal. When Donne writes of 'a bracelet of bright hair about the bone' or when Marvell states that 'The grave's a fine and pleasant place', there is a brutality in the juxtaposition of the ugly and the beautiful. In Synge the brutality may emerge from the clash of literary language with the vernacular. It may also arise from the clash of the romantic and the Rabelaisian. Synge used this technique quite consciously. Of a critic who preferred *Riders to the Sea* to *The Playboy,* he wrote; 'I don't think he sees that the romantic note and a Rabelaisian note are working to a climax through a great part of the play, and that the Rabelaisian note, the 'gross' note, if you will, *must* have its climax no matter who may be shocked.' *(Plays* II, p. xxv) Finally, there is a brutality in Synge's juxtaposing of the comic and the tragic; with the exceptions of *Riders to the Sea* and *Deirdre of the Sorrows* Synge's plays are tragicomedies where he deliberately wrenches and distorts the conventions of tragedy and comedy. Yeats was attracted – and puzzled – by this aspect of Synge's art.

41

'The strength that made him delight in setting the hard virtues by the soft, the bitter by the sweet, salt by mercury, the stone by the elixir, gave him a hunger for harsh facts, for ugly surprising things, for all that defies our hope.' *(Poems,* p. xxxiv)

Synge differs from Yeats also in that he never wavered in his belief that the Irish dramatic movement and the Abbey Theatre should seek to develop an Irish tradition of playwrights and acting. When Yeats, in 1906, raised the possibility of developing the Abbey Theatre along the lines of continental municipal theatres which performed the great classics, Synge objected forcibly:

> So far our movement has been entirely creative – the only movement of the kind I think now existing – and it is for this reason that it has attracted so much attention. To turn this movement now – for what are to some extent extrinsic reasons – into an executive movement for the production of a great number of foreign plays of many types would be, I cannot but think, a disastrous policy. . . . I think that Yeats' view that it would be a good thing for Irish audiences – *our* audiences – or young writers is mistaken.[12]

In 1898 Synge had listened to Yeats's views on the proposed new theatre movement; now, eight years later, his views prevailed and the Abbey Theatre received its stamp from his folk drama and not from the ideals and practice of Yeats. 'Yet we did not set out to found this sort of theatre,' Yeats wrote to Lady Gregory many years later, 'and its success has been to me a discouragement and a defeat.'[13]

When the Irish Literary Theatre launched its first season in 1899 the plays were performed by English actors, as was the case in the next two years. Whether Synge, who attended a performance of Yeats's *The Countess Cathleen* on 12 May of that year, saw the incongruity in English actors performing such plays we do not know. But Frank J. Fay, a reviewer for *The United Irishman*, did.

> What I want to know is why the conductors of the Irish Literary Theatre who pooh-pooh the ordinary English commercial Theatre cannot entrust the performance of their plays dealing with Irish subjects to a company of Irish actors. . . . It is manifestly the duty of those who will benefit by the Irish Literary Theatre plays to train up a company of Irish actors to do the work they want. Antoine did it in Paris.[14]

The Fay brothers were enormously talented men of the theatre who made an important contribution to the creation of an indigenous Irish dramatic movement. Frank Fay was a clerk stenographer with a firm of accountants who had a deep love of the theatre and a passionate interest in the speaking of English. Yeats wrote of him that he knew 'more than any man I have ever known about the history of Speech on the Stage'.[15] His brother, William, learned his theatre craft as a 'fit-up' man and actor with various touring stock companies that travelled throughout the United Kingdom. He became an electrician but his main ambition was to produce plays and to act. He was especially gifted for comedy, but his roles in Synge's plays, where he created the parts of Bartley, the Tramp, Martin Doul and Christy Mahon, suggest his range and versatility. Although the various companies which the Fays founded in Dublin, beginning in 1891, employed amateur actors and played mostly farces *(Box and Cox, My Wife's Dentist*), the Fays were ardent Nationalists who hoped to found a national dramatic movement which would mirror Irish ideals and aspirations.

The Fays were greatly influenced by Continental models, usually French, which they adapted to Irish conditions. A key influence was André Antoine (1858–1943), founder of the Théàtre Libre. Antoine was not a professional actor (he had been refused admission to the Conservatoire), he employed amateur actors and used the simplest of props, he chose 'artistic' and experimental plays rather than commercial plays, and he championed the virtues of ensemble acting. The simplicity and directness of his style in acting and staging created a revolution in France and was widely imitated in other countries. Interestingly, Synge's diaries for the 1890s record that he paid only two visits to the theatre – one was to Antoine's theatre in Paris in 1898. The Fays were also influenced by the work of the French actor, Constant Coquelin (1841–1909), seeking perhaps in his classical approach and technical training a counterbalance to Antoine's naturalism. In his reviews in *The United Irishman* Frank Fay praised Coquelin's work on a number of occasions, approving especially the ensemble work of his company:

Thanks to the Conservatoire which since 1784 has supplied and trained the French actors, a company of thoroughly competent players, with a uniform mode and perfectly familiar with the traditional method of interpreting the classics of their stage, can easily be obtained in Paris, and such a company M. Coquelin brought with him. The result was an example of life-like playing which it would be almost impossible to get on the English stage. [16]

When Gabriel Fallon joined the Abbey Company as an actor, Frank Fay gave him a copy of Arthur Symon's book, *Plays, Acting and Music,* referring him especially to an essay, 'Coquelin and Molière'.

In marrying the naturalism of Antoine (which Yeats disliked) and the classicism of Coquelin, the Fays turned what seemed insurmountable difficulties to their advantage. They had little money so they simplified scenery and theatrical effects; the actors were amateurs and full-time working people so they cultivated simplicity of technique and speech. The last was most important and, under the direction of Frank Fay who was an unusually gifted speaker and teacher of elocution, those actors whom he trained – Arthur Sinclair, J. M. Kerrigan, the Allgood sisters and Maire Nic Shiubhlaigh among others – startled audiences with the beauty and clarity of their speech. Bourgeois, a contemporary observer, noted that the Irish players were taught to avoid 'unnatural gesticulation and stage "business"', they spoke quietly (the small theatres in which they played were unsuited for the prevailing declamatory style), when they took curtain calls they bowed and smiled. He noted also that the simplicity of the Abbey method was complemented by a corresponding simplicity of set, scenery and costume.[17]

By 1901, with the end of the three-year period of the Irish Literary Theatre's activities, Yeats was uncertain in what direction the dramatic movement should go. Edward Martyn, for example, believed that the Theatre's activities should be directed to putting on in Dublin the best of European drama. This was also the view of the nineteen-year-old James Joyce, who, in a vitriolic pamphlet, 'The Day of the Rabblement', attacked the new literary nationalism:

The official organ of the movement spoke of producing European masterpieces, but the matter went no further. . . . A nation which never advanced so far as a miracle play affords no literary model to the artist, and he must look abroad. Earnest dramatists of the second rank, Sudermann, Björnson and Giacosa, can write very much better plays than the Irish Literary Theatre has staged.[18]

The case for an Irish drama and theatre was argued by the Fays who, in letters to Yeats and in Frank Fay's reviews in *The United Irishman,* urged the committee of the Irish Literary Theatre to gather a new company of Irish actors and present plays written in English and Gaelic. When the Fays finally received permission to stage A. E.'s *Deirdre,* Yeats offered them his *Cathleen Ni Houlihan* which he had written for Maud Gonne. The results were a revelation to Dublin audiences and the critics. Yeats has recorded his impressions of the company. 'They showed plenty of inexperience, especially in the minor characters, but it was the first performance I had seen since I understood these things in which the actors kept still enough to give poetical writing its full effect upon the stage. I had imagined such acting, though I had not seen it.'[19] It is an interesting comment on the simplicity which was at the heart of the Fay method that Maire Nic Shiubhlaigh modelled her playing of Cathleen Ni Houlihan on the performance of Maud Gonne for whom this was the first and last role on stage. When the company, now known as The Irish National Theatre Society, played in London in May 1903, it was principally the acting which caught the critics' attention. A. B. Walkley of *The Times* commented admiringly on the speech and movement of the Irish players. 'We had never realized the musical possibilities of our language until we have heard these Irish people speak it.' 'As a rule they stand stock-still. The speaker of the moment is the only one who is allowed a little gesture. . . . The listeners do not distract one's attention by fussy "stage business," they just stay where they are and listen.'[20] Willie Fay later wrote:

Walkley, I think, was the only one who had the wit to see immediately what Frank and I were driving at – not, of course, in the purely peasant pieces but in the serious and poetic plays, viz. to enforce the most rigid economy of gesture and movement, to make the speaking quite abstract, and at the same time to keep a music in it by having all the voices harmonised.[21]

The first play by Synge which the Fays produced was *The Shadow of the Glen.* Willie Fay noted admiringly that it 'showed little sign of the 'prentice hand'. Fay writes that Synge had from the beginning a sure sense of the dramatic.

His power of visualisation was perfect. I would work out a scale plan of the stage and furniture, and he would say,'That is just the way I saw the room as I was writing the play.'. . . he knew what he wanted, and when he got it said so – which is a virtue rare in dramatic authors.[22]

Synge's power of visualization was complemented by an extraordinary ability to intensify a scene through gesture and detail. One thinks of Cathleen counting the stitches in *Riders to the Sea,* of Molly sitting in Mary's seat in the recognition scene of *The Well of the Saints,* of the elderly King Conchubor examining Deirdre's workbox in *Deirdre*

47

of the Sorrows. Hand in hand with this ability is Synge's sureness of dramatic touch in investing major scenes with a compelling theatricality. One might cite the funeral procession in *Riders to the Sea,* the drinking scene which closes *The Shadow of the Glen,* the sports competition on the sands in *The Playboy* with the mountain girls hooshing Christy on, the burning of Emain as Naisi and his brothers are slaughtered in *Deirdre of the Sorrows.*

The Fays's experience with the poetic plays of Yeats was of little help in mastering Synge's dialect and the rhythm of his speech. 'He and I soon got together,' Fay wrote, 'and experimented with the dialogue until, after much hard practice, I got at how the speeches were built up, and could say any of the lines exactly in the way he wanted.' Maire Nic Shiubhlaigh, who was to play Nora Burke to Willie Fay's Tramp, notes a similar difficulty in speaking Synge's lines. 'It was neither verse nor prose. The speeches had a musical lilt, absolutely different to anything I had heard before . . . I found I had to break the sentences – which were uncommonly long – into sections, chanting them, slowly at first, then quickly as I became more familiar with the words.'[23]

While the dramatist and his actors sought for authenticity of dialect and speech, they also sought for authenticity in costume and scenery and props. Synge insisted that the pampooties and flannel worn in *Riders to the Sea* be from Inishmaan, and he even suggested that Sara Allgood be taught to spin. It was probably in pursuit of such realism that the actresses in *Riders to the Sea* visited an old peasant woman living in Dublin in order to learn how the *caoine* should be sung. When Synge later became a director of the Irish National Theatre Society, his knowledge of theatre and its attendant business increased greatly. He helped recruit and train new actors, he mediated disputes in the company, he read new plays and offered advice to would-be dramatists. 'Often for months together he and I and Lady Gregory would see no one outside the Abbey Theatre,' Yeats remembered, 'and that life, lived as it were in a ship at sea, suited him.' The care with which he wrote his last three plays shows his heightened awareness of theatrical conventions and stage craft; the manuscripts show him constantly seeking to make his work more dramatic. Finally, he conducted the rehearsals of his own plays.

Before the opening of the Abbey Theatre the Irish dramatists had only the most primitive of stage facilities. Both *The Shadow of the Glen* and *Riders to the Sea,* for example, were produced at the Molesworth Hall which seated an audience of 300. The stage was small – a 17-foot proscenium with a depth of 12 feet. Since the hall was rented, it meant that rehearsals had to be held elsewhere, a great disadvantage. Miss A. E. Horniman's purchase of the Abbey Theatre marked an important step in the development of facilities that would enhance the work of the Abbey dramatists. 'I can only afford to make a very little Theatre,' she wrote to Yeats in 1904, 'and it must be quite simple. You all must do the rest to make a powerful and prosperous Theatre, with a high artistic ideal.'

The new theatre seated 178 persons in the stalls, 186 in the pit, 198 in the balcony. The lighting was by electricity and the stage itself was lit by foot and head reflectors that were used to reinforce the mood and action of the play. The proscenium opening was 21 feet, the width of the stage 40 feet, the depth a little over 16 feet.[24] The new theatre opened on 27 December 1904 with plays by Synge, Lady Gregory and Yeats. It was an event of enormous cultural significance, for it marked the emergence of an indigenous school of playwrights which would add honour to the tradition established by Anglo-Irish dramatists like Congreve, Farquhar, Sheridan, Goldsmith and Wilde; the actors of the Abbey company would also add lustre to a long Irish theatrical tradition which had given the stage such renowned actors as Quin, Macklin, Barry, Peg Woffington and the Sheridans. In 1912 the critic P. P. Howe wrote: 'By the time *The Playboy of the Western World* was presented, it is probable that the Abbey Theatre in Dublin was the best theatre – the theatre possessing in the highest perfection all the essentials of its art – in the English-speaking world.'[25]

4
'Riders to the Sea'

Riders to the Sea, Synge's first play, is an astonishingly mature work of art. Whether we regard it as literature or as drama (a distinction Synge liked to make), it is a masterpiece enjoyed equally in the library or in the theatre; the role of Maurya has a special cachet for actresses like that attached to playing Medea or Lady Macbeth or Hedda Gabler. Like all great works of art it defies definition, seeming inexhaustible in meaning and complexity. The plot is simplicity itself. Maurya, an old woman, hopes that the body of her son, Michael, will be washed ashore. He was drowned nine days earlier. Already Maurya has lost her husband, her father-in-law and four other sons to the sea. When the play opens her two daughters have been given clothes from the body of a drowned man. Before they can discover whether the clothes are Michael's, Bartley, the youngest son, enters preparing for a journey by sea to the Galway horse-fair. Despite the entreaties of his mother not to go, he sets off. 'He's gone now, God spare us,' his mother cries, 'and we'll not see him again.' It is as she says. The daughters identify the clothes of the drowned man as Michael's, and Bartley is knocked off his horse and drowned in the sea. In the last third of this remarkably short play Maurya mourns the death of her family and invokes mercy on all the living and the dead.

Although Synge's notebooks and letters tell us little about the origin and composition of *Riders to the Sea,* the central incident of the play and many of the motifs used in it are drawn from Synge's experiences on the Aran Islands on his last visit in 1901. The story on which the play is based and from which the play derives its title is told in Part Four of *The Aran Islands:*

> When the horses were coming down to the slip an old woman saw her son, that was drowned a while ago, riding on one of them. She didn't say what she was after seeing, and this man caught the horse, he caught his own horse first, and then he caught this one, and after that he went out and was drowned.

The difficulties in dramatizing such an incident, in making a modern audience accept a ghost story based on 'second sight', are formidable. Shakespeare posed the difficulty squarely in the opening scene of *Hamlet:*

> MARCELLUS: What, has this thing appear'd again tonight?
> BERNANDO: I have seen nothing.
> MARCELLUS: Horatio says 'tis but our fantasy
> And will not let belief take hold of him.

Synge secures from his audience a willing suspension of disbelief because he roots his theme of multiple death and terrifying prescience in a meticulous faithfulness to the details of everyday peasant life, while simultaneously investing those details with archetypal associations that have validity for an audience seemingly far removed from any experience of peasant life.

An incident recorded in Part Three of *The Aran Islands* helped Synge ground his 'ghost story'. 'Now a man has been washed ashore in Donegal with one pampooty on him, and a striped shirt with a purse in one of the pockets, and a box for tobacco.' This becomes the substance of the slender subplot relating to Michael's death, and by investing it with realistic detail, such as the business surrounding the identification of the bundle of clothes as Michael's, Synge masks the difficulties inherent in dramatizing the supernatural. In his handling of this subplot, and in having Nora and Cathleen voice their doubts (and ours) about the reality of Maurya's vision, Synge skilfully presents an appearance of objectivity and reasonableness that allays our tendency to disbelieve.

MAURYA: I seen Michael himself.
CATHLEEN: *(speaking softly)*. You did not, mother . . . .

This art by which Synge makes Nora and Cathleen surrender ultimately to Maurya's vision reveals how Synge moves between the literal reality of Aran life and a more elevated and richer reality of archetype and symbol. The island surrounded by the implacable, death-dealing sea is also the arena of man's struggle in a hostile and meaningless universe.

This simultaneity of Synge's art in this respect is clearly suggested by the props which dominate the set: nets, a spinning-wheel, new boards, a halter hanging on the wall. These are everyday Aran household items which persuade us that the action is naturalistic, but as the play unfolds they become charged with enormous symbolic voltage. When the play opens Cathleen finishes kneading bread and begins to spin. The stage directions reinforce unobtrusively that extraordinary sense of inevitability in the play on which nearly all critics comment.

> CATHLEEN: *(spinning the wheel rapidly)*. What is it you have?
> NORA: The young priest is after bringing them. It's a shirt and a plain stocking were got off a drowned man in Donegal.
> (CATHLEEN *stops her wheel with a sudden movement, and leans out to listen.*)

The abrupt stopping of the wheel intimates clearly that the clothes belong to Michael and that he is dead. The rope that the pig with the black feet was eating is used to lead a horse; but a halter or rope is also associated with death by hanging. The white boards are intended for Michael's coffin, not for new household furniture

The mood of the play which is suggested by the props and the opening stage directions is intensified also by the many references to storm, which intimate crisis and disorder. The play is dominated by the sound of the sea and allusions to the elements and the points of the compass. The two women discuss the impending storm as they prepare to identify the clothes of the drowned man:

> CATHLEEN: Is the sea bad by the white rocks, Nora?
> NORA: Middling bad, God help us. There's a great roaring in the west, and it's worse it'll be getting when the tide's turned to the wind.

The coming of the old woman, Maurya, forces the two women to postpone identifying the clothes and increases our desire to be convinced of what we already believe. The action now centres on Maurya's attempt to dissuade Bartley from going to the Galway fair. 'The young priest will stop him surely,' Maurya says, but Nora has already told Cathleen that the priest will not attempt to stop Bartley because he is convinced God will not take her last son. The dramatic irony here adumbrates a dominant and recurring theme in Synge's work – the opposition of Christian belief and older, pagan beliefs. The young priest, it is clearly intimated, is powerless in the face of the eternal and malignant sea. The drowning of the last surviving son is bitter testimony to the immeasurable cruelty of the god of the Aran islanders. The point is made more explicitly in the first completed draft of the play where the time is Martinmas, the old feast of Mars, god of slaughter. 'In three nights it is Martin's night and it is from this house a sheep must be killed.' Maurya herself dismisses the young priest's assurance. 'It's little the like of him knows of the sea. . . . Bartley will be lost now.'

The tragic inevitability which marks the opening of the play extends to the scene between Maurya and Bartley. Bartley acts like a man driven to carry out a predestined task and Maurya's arguments seem curiously inadequate, even obtuse. She asks him not to take the rope which will be needed for Michael's funeral and she points out that he is needed for the task of burying his brother. Her concern seems primarily directed at observing the proprieties due to the dead. Only in her third speech to Bartley does she speak of his possible death, and not of Michael's actual death. 'If it was a hundred horses, or a thousand horses you had itself, what is the price of a thousand horses against a son where there is one son only?'

J. M. Synge

The inability of mother and son to communicate – their enmity even – is further emphasized by the fact that Maurya refuses to give Bartley her blessing even though she knows he is going to his death. Similarly, it is suggested that she, the mother, withholds from Bartley the bread that might have sustained him. 'You're taking away the turf from the cake,' Nora reproaches Maurya and sends her off to give Bartley the blessing she has withheld.

The daughters now identify the clothes as belonging to the dead Michael because of the four dropped stitches. In this scene Synge works skilfully on two levels. Although the primary interest in the play is directed to Bartley and his fate, Michael dominates the play, and the various clues that lead to the establishment of his death help to establish Bartley's death. No sooner do Cathleen and Nora establish Michael's death than Maurya enters keening because she claims to have seen 'the fearfullest thing' – her son Michael riding the grey horse. The *peripeteia* or reversal which Synge has managed here – in apparent contradiction to the literal truth – is linked to a stunning recognition *(anagnorisis)* which is that Bartley will die. The finest kind of recognition is accompanied by simultaneous *peripeteia,* as in the *Oedipus,* Aristotle claims. The effect Synge achieves here in relating *peripeteia* and recognition is among the most theatrical of his entire work.

The sequence leading up to Bartley's death contains many clues about the meaning of the play. Maurya, carrying Michael's stick, sets out for the spring (where she gets Holy Water 'in the dark nights after Samhain') to meet Bartley. Bartley, wearing Michael's clothes, blesses his mother, but she is unable to offer him the life-sustaining bread or return his blessing. 'I could say nothing.' It is then she sees Michael arrayed in new clothes riding the grey pony and she recognizes that her last son must die. 'Bartley will be lost now.' On hearing of Michael's ghostly apparition Cathleen, who had earlier denied that he was living, immediately accepts the truth of Maurya's vision. Her *volte face* is immediate and unconditional. The grey pony seems an analogue of the allegorical 'pale horse' of the Apocalypse ('And I looked, and behold, a pale horse: and his name that sat on him was Death, and Hell followed with him'). It is to the non-literal reality of the grey pony that the three women respond and we can be sure that this was the effect Synge intended. For example, the ship which comes to bear Bartley away is a very real ship which is mentioned three times and always with reference to 'the green head'. But the fact that Synge is very specific about the ship's location does not preclude suggestions that this is a death ship come for Bartley. *The Aran Islands* tells of two fairy ships one of which sought to lure a man to his death at a 'green point' and one which is associated with 'a great flock of birds on the water and they all black'. The storyteller specifically seeks a symbolic relationship between ship and bird. '" I think those black gulls and the ship were the same sort."' In a further equation the black gulls emerge in *Riders to the Sea* as 'the black hags that do be flying on the sea' over the dead Michael. Nets, halter, wheel, boards, ships, horses – Synge has woven a complex nexus of images that suggest entrapment, futility and death.

In *The Aran Islands* most of the many stories about horses appeal to the supernatural. A young woman who was stolen by the fairies describes a gathering or hosting. 'Then she told them they would all be leaving that part of the country on the Oidhche Shamhna, and that there would be four or five hundred of them riding on horses, and herself would be on a grey horse, riding behind a young man.' Another story tells of a man who heard someone riding on the road behind him. 'The noise behind him got bigger as he went along as if twenty horses, and then as if a hundred or a thousand, were galloping after him.' Later the priest tells the storyteller, 'it was the fallen angels'. The horses of *Riders to the Sea,* like the riders of the title, suggest at once scenes from the actual life of the Aran people while intimating through myth and symbol more universal dimensions. The spectral and apocalyptic rider on the grey pony that Maurya saw has associations with the ghostly riders in the folk stories recounted in *The Aran Islands* and with the horsemen of *Revelations* and especially the pale horse; on the literal and mythic levels the rider represents death which is why the mother cried out in fear when she saw him. Michael is one of the company of the dead who comes seeking out his brother to join the fairy company just as the fairies stole the young women in the story in *The Aran Islands.* We might go further and argue that for some mysterious reason Michael murders his brother. 'It is the ghostly Michael who is the killer of his younger brother – for reasons that lie deep in the Irish psychology'.[1] This fratricide is the first of those complex psychological and familial conflicts that Synge explored in his plays. *The Shadow of the Glen,* like *Riders to the Sea,* is dominated by a corpse – in this case a husband symbolically killed by his wife. In *The Well of the Saints* husband and wife threaten to kill each other in a scene of startling realism immediately following their 'cure'; the theme of *The Playboy* is parricide. Deirdre and Naisi quarrel bitterly immediately before he is killed. 'It's women that have loved are cruel only,' Naisi declares. In the *Poetics* Aristotle states that the terrible and pitiful incidents proper to tragedy arise when suffering is caused by people whose relationship implies affection, as when a brother kills a brother, a son his father, a mother her son, a son his mother.

The remainder of the play, following Maurya's account of her meeting with Bartley and Michael, is an extended threnody or dirge in which Synge heightens the ritualistic character of the drama and combines narration (the threnody) with enactment (the procession of mourners with the corpse of Bartley). Past and present merge as in a dream-sequence while the mother chants the name of her dead 'men-children' (Bourgeois's phrase),[2] and the enactment of one man's death becomes an image of every man's death:

> There was Patch after was drowned out of a curagh that turned over. I was sitting here with Bartley, and he a baby, lying on my two knees, and I seen two women, and three women, and four women coming in, and they crossing themselves, and not saying a word. I looked out then, and there were men coming after them, and they holding a thing in the half of a red sail, and water dripping out of it – it was a dry day, Nora – and leaving a track to the door. (*Plays* I, p. 21)

It is one of the finest speeches in the play; Maurya, *mater dolorosa,* remembers Bartley as a baby, while the man Bartley now reduced to 'a thing' is borne in. The sea, like a malevolent animal, tracks its victim even into the heart of the family. Past, present and the future coalesce to give a quality of timelessness and dream which is intensified by the sense of ordered ritual that prevails. The keening women take their prescribed place in a frieze of ceremonial grief; the daughters kneel at the one end of the table on which the corpse is laid. The mother, at the head of the table or altar, is like a priestess about to celebrate the last rites as she begins her last great speech, 'They're all gone now, and there isn't anything more the sea can do to me. . . .'

Since the meaning of Maurya's final speeches is central to an understanding of *Riders to the Sea,* it is helpful if we define more clearly the genre of the play. If *Riders to the Sea* is a tragedy (which some critics doubt), it is clearly not a tragedy in the Greek or Shakespearean sense of the word. In both Greek and Shakespearean tragedy the unhappy catastrophe is brought about by causally related events associated with the protagonist's 'flaw' or *harmartia.* But *Riders to the Sea* differs radically in that there is no causality which dictates a fitting punishment; Michael and Bartley are the victims of an arbitrary fate and it is because of this arbitrariness that the play is closer to irony than to tragedy. And in what sense can the drowned men of *Riders to the Sea* be said to have a 'flaw'? Maurya (and Michael and Bartley) are too passive in their suffering and because of this they are scapegoats or *pharmakoi,* rather than protagonists. 'The archetype of the inevitably ironic is Adam,' Northrop Frye writes, 'human nature under sentence of death.'[3] One is reminded of what Synge wrote after witnessing the harrowing burial scene on his last visit to the Aran Islands: 'As they talked to me and gave me a little poteen and a little bread when they thought I was hungry, I could not help feeling that I was talking with men who were under a judgement of death.'

We might also contrast Synge's play with Greek and Shakespearean tragedy in terms of the moral vision it establishes. Greek and Shakespearean tragedy is based on a system of values. Gilbert Murray writes that 'the ritual on which tragedy was based embodied the most fundamental Greek conception of life and fate, of law and sin and punishment.'[4] Shakespearean tragedy affords us a complex vision of good and evil; in some cases evil may appear to win out over good, but the action, nevertheless, is always conducted within a value system or moral order. Dennis Donoghue argues that *Riders to the Sea* is not a tragedy because it lacks a significant equivalent of 'the valued'; it fails to give a sense of heightened life; Maurya is an unconvincing protagonist because her sufferings are determined 'by forces which do not include her will or her character'.[5]

And yet it may be argued that there is a 'value', a 'good', in the play which has been obscured or passed over because critics have been reluctant to modify traditional definitions of tragedy. The 'good' in *Riders to the Sea* is death itself. The play expresses fear and apprehension about living and dying, but never about a death which is attended by proper observance. The young priest offers comfort by stating that Michael has had 'a clean burial'; the rope to lower the coffin is 'new'; Maurya hopes to give Michael 'a deep grave . . . by the grace of God' and she has given 'a big price for the finest white boards you'd find in Connemara'. The tension in the scene between Maurya and Bartley arises partly from the fact that he may somehow thwart the burial that has been prepared for Michael. Cathleen echoes the mother's horror that Michael will not receive a proper burial. 'Ah, Nora, isn't it a bitter thing to think of him floating that way to the far north, and no one to keen him but the black hags that do be flying on the sea?' Later Cathleen, to comfort her mother, contradicts this statement when she says that Michael did get 'a clean burial, by the grace of God'. The imagery of Maurya's last speeches confirms this notion of death as a good. Michael, angel of death, wears 'fine' clothes and 'new shoes', the coffin for Bartley will be 'a good coffin out of the white boards'. The substance of those speeches should also be taken at face value; they speak of something won, rather than something lost; they are not speeches of despair or acceptance or resignation, but speeches of acquiescence, even justification. Birth is hard, life a trial to be endured, death a deliverance.

> MAURYA: . . . Michael has a clean burial in the far north, by the grace of the Almighty God. Bartley will have a fine coffin out of the white boards, and a deep grave surely. . . . What more can we want than that? . . . No man at all can be living for ever, and we must be satisfied.

This is reminiscent of the sentiment voiced by the chorus at the close of *Oedipus Rex:*

> Call no man fortunate that is not dead.
> The dead are free from pain.

It echoes too the sentiments voiced by Martin MacDonough in a letter to Synge: 'it fell out that the wife of my brother Seaghan died, and she was buried the last Sunday of the month of December and look! that is a sad story to tell, but if it is itself, we must be satisfied because nobody can be living forever.'[6]

But while the sentiments in both *Oedipus Rex* and this letter are reminiscent of that of Maurya's final speech, Synge's play is grounded on a metaphysical view of the universe far more pessimistic than Sophocles' or that expressed by MacDonough, which must be placed within the context of Christian belief in Resurrection. The passivity of Synge's characters and the arbitrariness of their fate suggest strongly that suffering has no redemptive or liberating role. In his fragmentary verse play, *Luasnad,*

Capa and Laine (begun in 1902), Luasnad, a fisherman, presents a terrifying picture of life's pain and the maliciousness of the gods:

> All this life has been a hurtful game
> Played out by steps of anguish. Every beast
> Is bred with fearful torment in the womb
> And bred by fearful torments in life-blood.
> Yet by a bait of love the aimless gods
> Have made us multitudes.

(Plays, I, p. 200)

The traditional attitude had been otherwise. 'Whatever its nature and whatever its apparent cause, his [man's] suffering had a meaning, it corresponded, if not always to a prototype, at least to an order whose value was not contested.'[7] But Synge contests this point of view; for him life has no dignity or significance 'only a bit of wet flour we do have to eat, and maybe a fish that would be stinking' *(Plays,* I, p.25); suffering leads to apathy, even callousness, rather than to compassion – 'I won't care what way the sea is when the other women will be keening.' *(Plays,* I, p. 25) 'We, who have experienced Shakespeare and Racine,' writes Northrop Frye, 'can add the corollary that tragedy is something bigger than four phases of Greek drama.'[8] Our experience of Synge will suggest a further corollary – that he too has amplified the definition of tragedy. Death is a 'good' because it liberates one from a meaningless, and therefore terrifying, existence. The sea is the symbol of an implacable and ravenous mortality which makes existence meaningless when traditonal humanist and Christian beliefs are jettisoned. Synge, in *Riders to the Sea,* has written a play that anticipates existentialism in its nihilism and in its denial of meaning. Some forty years later Beckett will sound the same note of existential despair. It is the burden of Lucky's great monologue in *Waiting for Godot:* 'the earth in the great cold the great dark the air and the earth abode of stones in the great cold alas alas . . . '

If *Riders to the Sea* is read in this light, we may wish to redefine the role of the three women in the play. Certainly they mourn the deaths of the Aran fishermen, but they also preside over those deaths. In *Riders to the Sea* only men die; the women endure. Maurya, spokeswoman for all three, justifies those deaths and acquiesces in them. The women endure because behind Cathleen, Nora and Maurya there may be faintly discerned those archetypal agents of the Greek *ananke* or *moira* – Clotho, Lachesis and Atropos, the three Fates.[9]

The parallels are neither exact–nor mathematical, but they are strong enough to suggest the presence in the play of this powerful myth. The three Fates or Moirai presided over birth, marriage and death: the thread of life is spun on Clotho's spinning-wheel, it is measured by the rod of Lachesis, it is cut by the shears of Atropos. The myth, writes Robert Graves, 'is based on the custom of weaving family and clan marks into a newly-born child's swaddling bands, and so allotting him his place in society.'[10] When *Riders to the Sea* opens Cathleen's rapid spinning is interrupted by Nora's news that they must identify the clothes of a drowned man. Cathleen immediately stops her wheel *'with a sudden movement'*. Later she cuts the string binding the clothing with a sharp knife and her sister identifies the clothes as Michael's because she had dropped four stitches thus giving them a 'family' mark. The mother, Maurya, withholds the bread of life because Bartley's allotted time has come – he is setting out on a journey; the ghost ship awaits him; he is in Michael's clothes; he is being stalked by Michael, the angel of death on the grey pony. In the scene between Maurya and Bartley, explanation or apology is irrelevant because both are playing roles already established. Maurya is the prescient seer, Bartley the predestined victim. Bartley is still standing in the doorway when Maurya foretells his death. 'He's gone now, God spare us, and we'll not see him again.' Knowing this she cannot give him the bread or her blessing. It is only after Bartley's death, in which she co-operates, that she can finally give him her blessing. 'May the Almighty God have mercy on Bartley's soul.' The actress Maire Ni Shiubhlaigh, who played in the original production of the play which was supervised by Synge, describes Maurya as 'an old woman counting the loss of her sons with a bitter satisfaction.'[11]

In redefining the role of the three women, and especially Maurya's role, we realize that Maurya is not the protagonist of the plays. Maurya's 'child-men' represent the protagonist and if they seem too passive for tragedy it is because they have no defence against the mortality represented by the ever-present sea. *Riders to the Sea* is a counterblast to Yeats's *Cathleen Ni Houlihan*. In Yeats's play the old woman calls the young men of Ireland to their death, but she also promises them immortality:

> They shall be remembered for ever,
> They shall be alive for ever,
> They shall be speaking for ever,
> The people shall hear them for ever.

But Synge is not one of the last Romantics: he is modern in his irony and in his unbelief and in his alienation. His victims stand in stark contrast to Yeats's heroic martyrs. 'And isn't it a pitiful thing when there is nothing left of a man who was a great rower and fisher, but a bit of an old shirt and a plain stocking?' Maurya, the querulous, bitter old woman, is no queenly Cathleen Ni Houlihan; she is more akin to Mrs Moore, the old lady in E. M. Forster's *A Passage to India,* who had arrived at the state where 'the horror of the universe and its smallness are both visible at the same time.' The echo in the Marabar Caves speaks of the same nihilism that makes Maurya long for sleep and oblivion: 'the echo began in some undescribable way to undermine her hold on life. Coming at the moment when she chanced to be fatigued, it had managed to murmur, "Pathos, piety, courage – they exist, but are identical, and so is filth. Everything exists, nothing has value."'[12] Mrs Moore's journey to India is a *rite de passage* in which she comes to realize the essential irrationality of the universe. Synge, in attendance at a burial on the Aran Islands, believed he heard a similar realization in the keening of the Aran islanders. 'This grief of the keen is no personal complaint for the death of one woman over eighty years, but seems to contain the whole passionate rage that lurks somewhere in every native of the island.' Maurya, however, shows nothing of this passionate rage – 'She's quiet now and easy,' Nora observes – only bitter satisfaction that she has seen her menfolk to their death. 'They're all together this time, and the end is come.'

Northrop Frye notes that man's entry into nature is an entrance into the existentially tragic. 'Merely to exist is to disturb the balance of nature. Every natural man is a Hegelian thesis, and implies a reaction; every new birth provokes the return of an avenging death. This fact, in itself ironic and now called *Angst,* becomes tragic when a sense of a lost and originally higher destiny is added to it.'[13] It is a limitation of *Riders to the Sea* (which makes the play a pathetic rather than a tragic experience) that Synge's metaphysical nihilism deprives his protagonists of any sense of a lost or higher destiny. Synge did come to understand that the artist might give meaning and pattern to this 'pragmatical, preposterous pig of a world'[14] and with increasing insight he embodied this understanding within the tragicomic perspectives of the succeeding plays.

5
The Wicklow Plays

The Shadow of the Glen, like *Riders to the Sea,* is based on
a story Synge heard on the Aran Islands, but the play
receives its atmosphere and characters from the hills and
glens of County Wicklow, which is south of Dublin and
within easy cycling reach of the capital. It was an area well
known to Synge since his childhood. In the Autobiography he writes, 'To wander as I did for years through the
dawn of night with every nerve stiff and strained with
expectation gives one a singular acquaintance with the
essences of the world.' The 'essences of the world', as
presented in Synge's essays on the Wicklow countryside
and its people, resemble – though in a muted, more
elegiac tone – those presented in *Riders to the Sea.* Here,
too, nature is hostile, and the people are continually
haunted by thoughts of death. *The Shadow of the Glen*
lacks the epic quality of *Riders to the Sea* but, in com-
pensation, Synge adds a psychological dimension lacking
in the earlier play. In *The Shadow of the Glen* we find
more human problems plaguing the men and women of

the glens – depression, loneliness, madness. They allude
continually, Synge writes, 'to the three shadowy countries
that are never forgotten in Wicklow – America (their El
Dorado), the Union and the Madhouse'.

The Wicklow essays are dominated by themes of death
and mutilation. 'An Autumn Night in the Hills' opens
with an account of the wounding of a dog and closes with
the homecoming of the corpse of a young mother, Mary
Kinsella, who had spent some time in the asylum. In
another essay, 'The Oppression of the Hills', excitement
seizes a man who has just drunk some whisky; he tears off
his clothes and runs naked into the hills where his body,
almost devoured by the crows, is later found. These
themes of death and mutilation are presented within a
landscape of terrifying claustrophobia and psychological
tension:

> Among the cottages that are scattered through the hills
> of County Wicklow I have met with many people who
> show in a singular way the influence of a particular
> locality. These people live for the most part beside old
> roads and pathways where hardly one man passes in the
> day, and look out all the year on unbroken barriers of
> heath. At every season heavy rains fall for often a week
> at a time, till the thatch drips with water stained to a
> dull chestnut and the floor in the cottages seems to be
> going back to the condition of the bogs near it. Then the
> clouds break, and there is a night of terrific storm from
> the south-west – all the larches that survive in these
> places are bowed and twisted towards the point where
> the sun rises in June – when the winds come down
> through the narrow glens with the congested whirl and
> roar of a torrent, breaking at times for sudden moments
> of silence that keep up the tension of the mind. At such

times the people crouch all night over a few sods of turf
and the dogs howl in the lanes.   *(Prose,*p. 209)

In the same essay, 'The Oppression of the Hills', Synge
explicitly equates physical and psychological landscape:

This peculiar climate, acting on a population that is
already lonely and dwindling, has caused or increased a
tendency to nervous depression among the people, and
every degree of sadness, from that of the man who is
merely mournful to that of the man who has spent half
his life in the madhouse, is common among these hills.

It was within this extraordinary Wicklow landscape (as
Synge perceived it) that he chose to dramatize the story of
the unfaithful wife which Pat Dirane had told him on his
first visit to the Aran Islands. The shanachie or storyteller
tells of seeking shelter in a cottage late at night. When he
is admitted by the woman of the house he sees a corpse
and all made ready for a wake. The shanachie is left with
the corpse while the woman goes out to spread the news of
her husband's death. The 'corpse' revives and tells the
shanachie he is pretending to be dead in order to catch his
wife with her lover. The woman returns with a young man
and sends him into the bedroom where she later joins him.
The husband takes a stick, enters the bedroom, and hits
the lover 'so that his blood lept up and hit the gallery'. In
Synge's version the shanachie becomes the Tramp, the old
man and his young wife are characterized as Dan Burke
and Nora Burke, the lover is an ineffectual young
shepherd named Michael Dara. He is contrasted with a
former lover of Nora – one Patch Darcy, a powerful and
virile shepherd who had recently gone mad and died.
Synge's play differs from the folk tale in that the adultery

and the murder of the lover are omitted, and at its conclusion Nora, driven out of her home by her husband, is forced to seek a new life with the Tramp.

Given the setting and the atmosphere of the Wicklow countryside where the action of *The Shadow of the Glen* takes place, it might seem surprising that Synge should introduce into his play a strain of comedy lacking in the bare and factual account given by Pat Dirane. Dan Burke, the husband, is a stark figure of comedy (even farce); the business surrounding him – his resurrection, his thirst for the whisky provided for his own wake, his presence during the 'love scene' where Michael Dara's wooing of Nora Burke is given ironic overtones by the counting of the husband's money (now Nora's dowry), the sneeze and the leap from the deathbed – all this is the stuff of comedy. But if it is comedy, it is comedy of a different kind from that, say, which we see in Molière's *Le Malade Imaginaire* (which features the same central incident). The novelty in Synge's work lies in the fact that he sympathizes with – and directs his audience's sympathy to – the outcast and the tramp, rather than to the respectable citizen and bourgeois farmer. Comic writing traditionally upholds the 'normal' and the established against the outsider, the outcast and the criminal. 'At the end of each of Synge's comedies, however, although the solid citizen is left in command of the stage, our hearts go with the outcasts.'[1]

The opening scene of the play demonstrates very clearly the down-to-earth, naturalistic nature of Nora. The Tramp is startled when he discovers that there is a corpse in the room, but Nora seems unconcerned – even callous. 'It doesn't matter any way,' she shrugs. Her next statement is one that might seem better fitted for such materialistic people as her husband or Michael Dara. 'He's after dying on me, God forgive him, and there I am now with a hundred sheep beyond on the hills, and no turf drawn for the winter.'

This opening scene also emphasizes Nora's sexuality. She says of her husband, 'he was always cold, every day since I knew him, – and every night, stranger.' She offers the Tramp whisky and her husband's pipe and tobacco. When, at this point in the play, she speaks of loneliness, her mood is sexually suggestive rather than melancholic. When the Tramp says that most women, on such a dark night, would be afraid of him, Nora retorts, 'I'm thinking many would be afeared, but I never knew what way I'd be afeared of beggar or bishop or any man of you at all.' References to Patch Darcy reinforce the sexual nature of the scene for he represents – among other things – virility. Nora speaks of him sorrowfully, lowering her voice as she looks at the bed where her husband is lying. 'God spare Darcy, he'd always look in here and he passing up or passing down.' A reference at this point to Michael Dara is beautifully placed. He is first pictured by the Tramp as being unable to control 'a drift of mountain ewes'; later, Michael Dara, with unconscious sexual innuendo, says:

> They were that wilful they were running off into one man's bit of oats, and another man's bit of hay, and tumbling into the red bogs till it's more like a pack of old goats than sheep they were . . . Mountain ewes is a queer breed, Nora Burke, and I'm not used to them at all.

When the Tramp joins Nora in praise of the dead Patch Darcy, they refer specifically to his great skill in handling mountain ewes. The sexuality associated with Patch Darcy and mountain ewes links the Tramp and Nora and suggests that, especially on Nora's part, there is a strong

1 J.M. Synge by J.B. Yeats

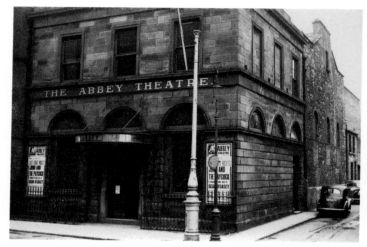

2a The Old Abbey Theatre

2b The interior of the Old Abbey Theatre

3 W.B. Yeats

Actresses of the Abbey Theatre

4b Sarah Allgood by Sarah Purser

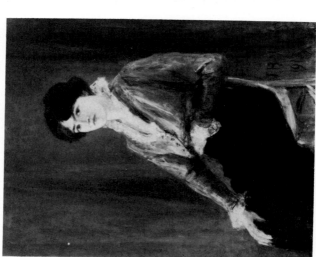

4a Maire O'Neill by J.B. Yeats

Actors of the Abbey Theatre

5a W.G. Fay by J.B. Yeats

5b Frank Fay by J.B. Yeats

6a Maire O'Neill, Sarah Allgood and Bridget Dempsey in *Riders to the Sea*
    (1906)

6b Eamon Kelly, Pat Laffan and Maire Ni Dhomhnaill in *The Well of the Saints*
    (1969)

7a Willie Fay in *The Shadow of the Glen*

7b Maire O'Neill in *Deidre of the Sorrows* (1910).

8 Siobhan McKenna and Cyril Cusack in *The Playboy of the Western World*
(1954)

sexual attraction towards the Tramp.

This attraction is further emphasized by the jealousy Michael Dara and the Tramp show towards each other. Dara disparages the Tramp's clothes, and the Tramp disparages Dara's skill in handling 'a little handful of ewes'. This further reference to the symbolic ewes leads Michael Dara to question Nora about her relations with Patch Darcy.

> MICHAEL: *(looking at her with a queer look)*. I heard tell this day, Nora Burke, that it was on the path below Patch Darcy would be passing up and passing down, and I heard them say he'd never pass it night or morning without speaking with yourself.
>
> NORA: *(in a low voice)*. It was no lie you heard, Michael Dara.
>
> MICHAEL: *(as before)*. I'm thinking it's a power of men you're after knowing if it's in a lonesome place you live itself.

Michael is clearly suggesting that Nora is what we would now call a sexually active woman and Nora does not deny the suggestion: ' . . . and if it's a power of men I'm after knowing they were fine men'.

If we pursue this aspect of the play we realize that when the husband charges that Nora is 'a bad wife for an old man', and speaks bitterly of Patch Darcy, he has indeed grounds for suspicion. This suspicion receives confirmation as the 'love scene' between Nora and Michael Dara progresses. The stage directions reinforce the scene's intent. Michael *'looks furtively at the bed, then draws closer to her'*; Nora pours him whisky and sits close to him; Michael *'puts his arms round her'*. Synge is here skirting the theme of adultery which is endowed with an added theatrical *frisson* because the scene is played in the presence of the husband and the Tramp.

We have, to this point, emphasized Nora's sexuality because too many critics have ignored it, preferring to follow Yeats's description of her as a woman 'melancholy as a curlew, driven to distraction by her own sensitiveness'.[2] This description seems at odds with the characterization adapted by Maire Nic Shiubhlaigh, the actress who created the role and who, presumably, had Synge's approval. Molly Allgood, who later played Nora, 'toned down the heroine's sexual ebullience',[3] but when C.E. Montague saw her in the part he wrote: 'you can feel the passion propel her like a screw.'[4] There is further evidence that Synge was fully aware that he was portraying an area of life – sexual activity – which was likely to offend. His friend, Stephen MacKenna, wrote that he would have preferred to see *The Shadow of the Glen* 'in book form, not on boards' on the grounds that 'modern problems even in peasant robes I do not like to see made public property in Ireland yet.' Synge's reply leaves no doubt that he considered the originality of *The Shadow of the Glen* resulted in large part from introducing sex to the Irish stage. 'On [the] French stage you get sex without its balancing elements. On [the] Irish stage you [get] the other elements without sex. I restored sex and the people were so surprised they saw the sex only.' Later, in the same letter Synge writes of Irish sexuality as he had never dared to in his articles: 'I have as you know perambulated a good deal in Ireland in my thirty [years] and if I were [to] tell, which Heaven forbid, all the sex horrors I have seen I could a tale unfold that would wither up your blood.'[5]

But if *The Shadow of the Glen* is a reflection of the sex horrors Synge had encountered in his travels, it also carries another thematic burden, one which reflects the loneliness, sadness and alienation mirrored in the essays. Within this context Nora is closer to Yeats's description of her as a woman 'melancholy as a curlew'; she is a creature intensely aware of the passing of time and the imminence of death. It is this tragic awareness that saves her from being merely a woman 'wearing her lusts upon her sleeve'; she is trapped by her realization that no matter what course she takes in life, none seems to offer her the freedom she craves.

The various alternatives offered Nora are shaped by the bitterness and squalidness of life in the Wicklow hills. When she tells Michael Dara that she is a hard woman to please, he retorts, 'Was it a hard woman to please you were when you took himself for your man?' He is refer-ring, of course, to the extreme difference in age between Nora and her husband; her answer underlines the stark economic realities of rural Irish marriages. 'What way would I live and I an old woman if I didn't marry a man with a bit of a farm, and cows on it, and sheep on the back hills?' But she has come to realize the futility of that alternative: ' . . . for what good is a bit of a farm with cows on it, and sheep on the back hills, when you do be sitting, looking out from a door the like of that door, and seeing nothing but the mists rolling down the bog?'

In the course of the play Nora is offered another alternative – marriage with a young man, Michael Dara, and the possibility of having children. This is the force of the reference to Mary Brien who is younger than Nora but has two children and is again pregnant. Yet this alterna-tive is undercut by her sense of mortality. 'Why would I marry you, Mike Dara? You'll be getting old, and I'll be getting old.' *(Plays* I, p. 51)

The most interesting possibility offered Nora – and it is one which she does not choose, but has forced upon her –

is the life offered her by the Tramp when she is rejected by her husband and lover. The Tramp is a complex figure who grew out of Synge's interest in the tramps he met in the Wicklow hills. A passage from 'The Vagrants of Wicklow' shows how Synge idealizes the type:

> In all the circumstances of this tramp life there is a certain wildness that gives it romance and a peculiar value for those who look at life in Ireland with an eye that is aware of the arts also. In all the healthy movements of art, variations from the ordinary types of manhood are made interesting for the ordinary man, and in this way only the higher arts are universal. . . . To be quite plain, the tramp in real life, Hamlet and Faust in the arts, are variations; but the maniac in real life, and Des Esseintes and all his ugly crew in the arts, are freaks only. *(Prose,* p. 208)

This idealized picture is greatly modified in *The Shadow of the Glen*. True, the Tramp does have something of the artist about him but he is no Christy Mahon. His final speeches where he bids Nora come with him are restrained and qualified. 'You'll be saying one time, "It's a grand evening by the grace of God," and another time, "It's a wild night, God help us, but it'll pass surely." ' This note of qualification had already been hinted at in the references to Patch Darcy. (It is noteworthy how absent figures – dead men – dominate three of Synge's plays: Michael in *Riders to the Sea,* Patch Darcy in *The Shadow of the Glen,* and old Mahon in *The Playboy.)* Admired by the Tramp and Nora, hated by Dan Burke, Patch Darcy is clearly meant to represent the healthy and the natural. Yet, though he is close to Nature, he goes 'queer in the head' and is eaten by crows. Peggy Cavanagh, it is also suggested, abandoned the horror of family life in the glens for the life of the vagrant, but ended in poverty and physical decay. The life of the road, of Nature, does not seem to provide an acceptable alternative; Dan Burke mocks Nora for her naive belief that it will offer her freedom, or hold back the ravages of time:

> Let her walk round the like of Peggy Cavanagh below, and be begging money at the cross roads, or selling songs to the men. *(To* NORA) Walk out now, Nora Burke, and it's soon you'll be getting old with that life, I'm telling you; it's soon your teeth 'll be falling and your head 'll be the like of a bush where sheep do be leaping a gap.

In a brutal speech he foretells her death (alike in its circumstances to Patch Darcy's death):

> It's lonesome roads she'll be going, and hiding herself away till the end will come, and they find her stretched like a dead sheep with the frost on her, or the big spiders, maybe, and they putting their webs on her, in the butt of a ditch. *(Plays* I, p. 55)

Some critics argue that the life of the Tramp offers hope to Nora. But it is difficult to accept this interpretation. The depression, hallucination and madness that characterize the people of the glens have been intensified – if not induced – by Nature. 'I have met with many people who show in a singular way the influence of a particular locality,' Synge writes. There is no evidence in the play that the Tramp has a wisdom superior to that of Patch Darcy or Peggy Cavanagh, or that he will not go the way of Patch Darcy. When he says, 'We'll be going now, lady of the house – the rain is falling but the air is kind, and maybe it'll be a grand morning by the grace of God', Nora's reply shows that she is painfully aware of the inadequacy of Nature to help her: 'What good is a grand morning when I'm destroyed surely, and I going out to get my death walking the roads?' The Tramp in his final speech seems to suggest that a life close to Nature offers some kind of immortality, that the songs of the birds somehow banish thoughts of growing old. But, if so, it is a claim that has already been undermined by the subtext which is dominated by the vagrant, Patch Darcy, who chose this way of life yet went mad and was destroyed.

> Come along with me now, lady of the house, and it's not my blather you'll be hearing only, but you'll be hearing the herons crying out over the black lakes, and you'll be hearing the grouse, and the owls with them, and the larks and the big thrushes when the days are warm, and it's not from the like of them you'll be hearing a talk of getting old like Peggy Cavanagh, and losing the hair off you, and the light of your eyes, but it's fine songs you'll be hearing when the sun goes up, and there'll be no old fellow wheezing the like of a sick sheep close to your ear.

Nora undercuts the Wordsworthian cast of this view of Nature. 'I'm thinking it's myself will be wheezing that time with lying down under the Heavens when the night is cold.' She goes with the Tramp, not because together they will prove the pleasures of Nature, but because the Tramp has 'a fine bit of talk'. Here is an alternative which is based on Synge's observation in the essay, 'The Vagrants of Wicklow', that there is an affinity between the tramp or vagrant and the artist, as earlier, in *The Aran Islands,* he had suggested that there was an affinity between the moods of the islanders and 'the moods of varying rapture and dismay that are frequent in artists, and in certain forms of alienation'. Synge's hint that the Tramp is, in some degree, a poet, that 'What the imagination seizes as Beauty must be truth – whether it existed before or not,'[6] is not explored in *The Shadow of the Glen*, however, and had to wait for fuller expression in *The Well of the Saints* and *The Playboy*. Because it is not explored more deeply in the play there is some truth to the charge that Synge's characterization of Nora is incongruous. In the opening scene of the play she is presented as being drawn sexually to the Tramp, although later, in the 'love scene' with Michael Dara, she seems prepared to marry him despite the fact that she is merely exchanging one form of servitude for another without even the excuse of poverty since she is now the inheritor of a prosperous farm. Were she, as in the folk tale, to choose a young lover whom she desires in preference to an old, impotent husband, her motivation would be clear. But she seems willing to marry Michael Dara for material reasons, and even after she is discovered by Dan Burke she offers to remain with him. Nora's willingness to settle for an old, impotent husband or for a young impotent husband – 'my lambs were the best lambs' – differs little from the peasant materialism of husband and putative lover; it seems to conflict with the sensitivity of character attributed to her by Yeats, which is appalled at the squalidness of domestic life and the certainty of physical decay, and seeks some kind of escape.

Synge, uninterested in the *pièce bien faite,* wished to leave the dénouement ambiguous because he was aware that there is no solution to what we might now term existential *Angst*. Nora's promiscuity (which is certainly implied) need not conflict with the deeper existential

J. M. Synge

burden of the play; now that we accept freer sexual mores than would have been permitted in Synge's age we may even recognize his originality and integrity in linking Nora's sexual promiscuity and melancholy despair. She is a trapped figure who would cling to her wretched existence (with Michael Dara, with Dan Burke) but is denied even that. In Ibsen's *A Doll's House* Nora Helmer rejects her husband and actively seeks her freedom. 'I must stand quite alone if I am to understand myself and everything about me. It is for that reason that I cannot remain with you any longer.' But Synge, rejecting what he held to be the sociological basis of Ibsen's problem plays (Nora Helmer is trapped because of her economic dependence on her husband), is concerned with psychological aspects of the *condition humaine*. Nora Burke's melancholy arises from her morbidly acute awareness of temporality; she is as mortality-ridden as Deirdre in Synge's last play. The bitterness and the poignancy of her situation are underlined by the fact that she lacks the courage to choose the life of the Tramp because she is realistic enough to realize that she will probably grow to be like Peggy Cavanagh.

The final scene of *The Shadow of the Glen* exemplifies powerfully the mordancy of Synge's comedy. Although in a letter to *The United Irishman* Synge stated that his play was not based on Petronius's tale of the widow of Ephesus, his letter reveals quite plainly that he was familiar with Petronius's account and a number of European variants on it. The final scene of *The Shadow of the Glen* may, in fact, owe something to the humorous cynicism of Petronius which is lacking in the Irish version. In Petronius's *Widow of Ephesus* the widow offers her seducer– soldier the body of her husband to replace the body of a crucified robber which had been stolen while under the soldier's care. Synge, with characteristic brutality, pushed the cynicism of the tale even further; in the place of Petronius's lovers feasting together in a conventionally happy dénouement he has the woman cast out upon the road while husband (Dan Burke) and 'lover' (Michael Dara) drink together. Synge is strikingly original in anticipating the tendency of contemporary dramatists (Ghelderode, Beckett, Ionesco, Frisch, Pinter) to re-form and re-create traditional genres. Ruby Cohn notes the difficulty critics have in defining plays of this nature: 'Karl Guthke finds in modern tragicomedy "reciprocity of the interaction of the tragic and the comic". Eric Bentley, on the other hand, suggests that the distinctively modern form of tragicomedy is 'comedy with an unhappy ending.'[7] This 'comedy with an unhappy ending' is nowhere more evident than in the magnificent closing scene of *The Shadow of the Glen* which, as Yeats noted, is the 'perfection of ironic humour':

> DAN: *(throwing away his stick)*. I was thinking to strike you, Michael Dara, but you're a quiet man, God bless you, and I don't mind you at all. *(He pours out two glasses of whisky, and gives one to MICHAEL)*.
> DAN: Your good health, Michael Dara.
> MICHAEL: God reward you, Daniel Burke, and may you have a long life and a quiet life, and good health with it.
> *(They drink)*

The Tinker's Wedding, the second of the Wicklow plays, was begun in the same year as *The Shadow of the Glen.* Synge dramatizes the comic predicament of a woman who enjoys the kind of freedom offered Nora by the Tramp but desires that church marriage which Nora rejects. If *The Shadow of the Glen* is an Irish and existential restatement of Ibsen's *A Doll's House, The Tinker's Wedding* is a comic and farcical rejoinder to *Hedda Gabler.*

Synge's play is based on a story recounted in the essay 'At a Wicklow Fair':

> One time he [a tinker] and his woman went up to a priest in the hills and asked him would he wed them for half a sovereign, I think it was. The priest said it was a poor price, but he'd wed them surely if they'd make him a tin can along with it. 'I will, faith,' said the tinker, 'and I'll come back when it's done.' They went off then, and in three weeks they came back, and they asked the priest a second time would he wed them. 'Have you the tin can?' said the priest. 'We have not, ' said the tinker; 'we had it made at the fall of night, but the ass gave it a kick this morning the way it isn't fit for you at all.' 'Go on now,' says the priest. 'It's a pair of rogues and schemers you are, and I won't wed you at all.' They went off then, and they were never married to this day.

What Synge did with this slight story was to turn it into a farce, the stuff for an *opera buffa,* in which caricature is as much in evidence as characterization, and where whimsy rather than reason dictates the improbable action. Synge retained the basic outline of the tale but he added an old tinker woman, Mary Byrne, Michael's mother. She sells the tin can meant for the priest for porter and replaces it with empty beer bottles. When, in Act II, the Priest discovers the trick he refuses to marry the young tinkers and threatens them with the police. They escape after tying him up in a sack.

Although no reason is given in the Wicklow story as to why the tinkers would want to get married, Synge chooses to stress this point. He does so because while the original story emphasized the roguery of the tinkers and only incidentally, if at all, the avarice of the priest, his purpose was to demonstrate the superiority of the tinkers' way of life and their 'natural' religion to that of the priest and the Church which he represents. The new character, Mary Byrne, becomes the sometimes too explicit spokeswoman for this point of view.

Sarah Casey's wish to regularize her relations with the man with whom she has been living, and by whom she has borne many children, would seem to be a normal and laudable thing to do. But it is Synge's purpose to show that marriage is an absurd institution and that Sarah is being merely wilful, if not unnatural. Sarah claims she wants to be married because it's springtime 'and it's queer thoughts maybe I do think at whiles.' Later she claims that marriage will give her that respectability she has been denied. 'I'll be married now in a short while; and from this day there will no one have a right to call me a dirty name and I selling cans in Wicklow or Wexford or the city of Dublin itself.' This speech suggests that Sarah is chafing at her tinker's life and its main occupation – selling tin cans. Dramatically (and on moral grounds) Synge seems to be leading his audience to sympathize with Sarah's wish to get married. The ring symbolises marriage, of course, but it suggests (to Sarah) something superior to her present way of life. Very early in the play, however, Synge begins to undermine Sarah's position. 'It's the divil's job making a ring,' Michael declares with unconscious irony, 'and you'll be having my hands destroyed in a short while the way I'll not be able to make a tin can at all maybe at the dawn of day.' When Sarah finally does try on the ring it hurts her. This contrast between the tin can and the ring becomes both a motif and a strong visual dramatic device throughout the play. The Priest will only marry the couple if he can have the tin can and this wish for the can is symbolic of his attraction to the tinkers' life and values:

> . . . it's well for the like of you that do be drinking when there's drouth on you, and lying down to sleep when your legs are stiff. *(He sighs gloomily.)* What would you do if it was the like of myself you were, saying Mass with your mouth dry, and running east and west for a sick call maybe, and hearing the rural people again and they saying their sins?

The Priest, a creation straight from the fabliaux of Boccaccio or Chaucer, may be a Christian by virtue of his calling but by nature he is as pagan as the tinkers. He is a card-player, a drinker, one who likes to sing songs till dawn, and, perhaps, a womanizer. 'You do be looking out and blinking at the girls,' Sarah scolds him. But if the Priest is pagan by nature and if, in fact, he is of a piece with old Mary Byrne, his natural spontaneity is perverted by his priestly office. He sings songs till dawn in the doctor's house, but he reproves Mary for singing, saying she would be better praying. Molly retorts with stinging irony, ' . . . I've heard a power of queer things and I walking the world, but there's one thing I never heard any time, and that's a real priest saying a prayer.'

It is Mary's function in the play to act as a foil to the Priest and to articulate for the audience the moral or 'message' of the action. She may spend her time getting drunk or cadging drinks, but Synge clearly means her to be representative of natural goodness and hence superior to those values represented by the Priest's office. When she first enters she sings a song which debunks the pretensions of the clergy:

And when we asked him what way he'd die,
   And he hanging unrepented,
'Begob,' says Larry, 'that's all in my eye,
   By the clergy first invented.'

It is Mary who, unwittingly, prevents the marriage by selling the tin can for porter. But her feelings about the proposed marriage are never in doubt. To her son she says, 'I never knew till this day it was a black born fool I had for a son.' Michael's defence of his foolishness further develops the comic incongruity that Synge is exploiting. He will marry Sarah, he says, but only because she makes him a great deal of money. 'If I didn't marry her, she'd be walking off to Jaunting Jim maybe at the fall of night; and it's well yourself knows there isn't the like of her for getting money and selling songs to the men.'

Synge's characterization of Mary has been much praised and certainly she is engaging in her humanity, her largeness, her bawdiness – a Wife of Bath almost. But she also threatens to become too obviously the mouthpiece of values not dramatically inherent in the text of the play or growing out of the interplay of character. We feel that Mary is speaking in character when she dismisses Sarah's wish to be married as 'fooling' and 'fussing' caused by 'the change of the moon'. But her later explanation for Sarah's behaviour seems out of character and threatens to undermine the farcicality of the play:

Is it putting that ring on your finger will keep you from getting an aged woman and losing the fine face you have, or be easing your pains, when it's the grand ladies do be married in silk dresses, with rings of gold, that do pass any woman with their share of torment in the hour of birth, and do be paying the doctors in the city of

Dublin a great price at that time, the like of what you'd pay for a good ass and a cart?

Mary is here the too-obvious mouthpiece for a theme that Synge has sounded in *The Shadow of the Glen* – the implacability of time and its destruction of beauty. But Sarah is not Nora Burke; she is a splendid creature of impulse and violence and to attribute, even indirectly, such an attitude to her is to do violence to her character – and to the play's genre.

Mary is also made the spokeswoman for the superiority of the tinker's way of life and its wildness to the restrictive and conventional morality of the Priest. In this respect too, we, the audience, may feel that Synge has palpable designs upon us. Mary counsels the Priest now tied in the sack:

> That's a good boy you are now, your reverence, and let you not be uneasy, for we wouldn't hurt you at all. It's sick and sorry we are to tease you; but what did you want meddling with the like of us, when it's a long time we are going our own ways – father and son, and his son after him, or mother and daughter, and her own daughter again – an it's little need we ever had of going up into a church and swearing – I'm told there's swearing with it – a word no man would believe, or with drawing rings on our fingers, would be cutting our skins maybe when we'd be taking the ass from the shafts.

The outcome of the clash between the Priest and the tinker is never in doubt because Synge's sympathies are clearly with the tinkers and the freedom they symbolize. Like Blake, Shelley and James Joyce, Synge is anticlerical and the evidence is everywhere in his work. The central incident of *When the Moon Has Set,* a play Synge worked on between 1896 and 1903, is the protagonist's successful attempt to make a young nun break her vow of celibacy and marry him. The wedding ceremony which he conducts is a parody of the Christian doxology: 'We have incarnated God, and been a part of the world. That is enough. *(He takes her hand.)* In the name of the Summer, and the Sun, and the Whole World, I wed you as my wife.' A fragment called 'Lucifer and the Lost Soul: A Mystery' contains this exchange (Maynooth is the major Catholic seminary for the education of priests in Ireland):

LUCIFER: And what brought [you] this place?
LOST SOUL: The way of the world, your reverence.
LUCIFER: Bad company.
LOST SOUL: The worst. In Maynooth I was with all nice little priests, talking ever and always of the deadly merits. I run from that.

Mary's speech to the Priest appears in a notebook draft in a much harsher form and leaves no doubt as to the original anti- clerical character of the play:

Is it rings we want when the frost does catch on our fingers. Let you listen to this. When a man parts with copper to put rings in a pig's nose and you'ld like us to pay you with the time you'ld put an old ring on ourselves. You would surely. Herself is a young woman and the young never know the things they want. I've had one husband and another husband and a power of children God help them and it's little they or myself even with your old rings to help us on in the world. Good day now your reverence ,and let you be putting

rings on your own pigs and not minding ourselves it's
ten generations I was saying we've been walking round
on the roads and never a marriage in the family.

(Plays II, pp. 276–7)

The trouble with speeches like these, which are echoed
in the finished play, is that they give it a didactic tone
which Synge in the preface to the play held to be alien to
the best drama. 'The drama, like the symphony, does not
teach or prove anything,' he wrote, and went on to praise
the plays of Jonson and Molière in this regard in contrast
to the work of Ibsen and the Germans. When the tinkers
attack the Priest and truss him in the sack, we do not mind
seeing the Priest so treated but we do object when the
same Priest is made to seem a representative of that
Christianity which Synge abhorred; he is too patent a butt.
The play is at its best when it exploits the unnaturalness of
Sarah in wishing to get married. To follow out the
consequences of that wish is to pursue the farcical and the
comical; to seek to prove its truth *à thèse* is to distort the
genre.

There is a further difficulty in trying to prove the
superiority of the tinkers' values to those of the Priest. It
goes against the grain of comedy, which usually buttresses
the normal and the established. But *The Tinker's Wedding*
asks its audience to reject the normal and the established –
marriage – as absurd, and while an audience may be
prepared temporarily to suspend moral judgement, it
expects an ultimate restatement of what it regards as
normal and moral. But Synge's return to the *status quo
ante* (Sarah as enlightened pagan) deflates that expectation; it is an ironic and characteristic stroke which anticipates the black comedy of our time. The distortion of the
genre caused by this stroke is, however, too strong for this

slight farce. Were Mary's role as didact understated, *The Tinker's Wedding* would play very well to audiences now grown accustomed to the absurdity of Ionesco and the metaphysical slapstick of Beckett. In *The Well of the Saints* and *The Playboy of the Western World* Synge continues to oppose human freedom to the restrictions of priest and church, but he does so without the didacticism that mars this work.

The Tinker's Wedding is, in final analysis, a slight play and is now seldom played in the theatre. The best things about it are the brilliantly etched portraits of the two women. Sarah in her beauty and wilfulness and violence anticipates Pegeen Mike, and there is more than a little of Mary's bawdiness and broad humanity in the Widow Quin. Finally, the play is an interesting and typical statement of Synge's concern with the subject of human liberty. Within the bitter perspectives of *The Shadow of the Glen* he shows how difficult it is for the individual to find freedom; in *The Tinker's Wedding* he shows how difficult it is for the individual who possesses freedom to recognize that it can easily be destroyed by convention and custom.

6
'The Well of the Saints'

Synge's first full-length play, *The Well of the Saints,* has been received with more enthusiasm by the critics than by audiences, which have preferred *Riders to the Sea* and *The Playboy.* It may be that, like the original Abbey players, they find the vision of the play too narrow and intense and the irony too Swiftian in its misanthropy (softened only in the final act). Willie Fay recorded his impression of the play:

> I realized that every character in the play from the Saint to Timmy the Smith was bad-tempered right through the play, hence, as I pointed out to Synge, all the bad temper would inevitably infect the audience and make them bad-tempered too. I suggested that the Saint anyway might be made into a good-natured, easy-going man, or that Molly Byrne might be made a lovable young girl, but Synge would not budge. He said he wanted to write 'like a monochrome painting, all in shades of the one colour'. [1]

Joseph Holloway, indefatigable diarist, records that 'The company, when they were rehearsing *The Well of the Saints* used to say the play made them sick.'[2] The play is certainly the most sombre and philosophic of all Synge's work, fusing a number of themes he had already sounded – the outsider versus society; the pagan versus the church and the priest; the clash of reality and dream, of truth and illusion. The same themes are sounded in *The Playboy of the Western World,* but in that play Synge exchanges the monochromatic colour scheme of *The Well of the Saints* for fervid colours of an almost Elizabethan exuberance in order to portray a far broader range of character, emotion and situation.

The Well of the Saints is a black comedy about two blind, married beggars, Martin Doul and Mary Doul ('Doul' is the Gaelic for 'blind'), who have their sight restored to them by a holy man. But rather than finding happiness, they become more miserable. They quarrel, drift apart, but when blindness again returns they become reconciled and abandon the gross world of reality for a world of illusion consciously chosen. Synge came across the central incident when taking a course in medieval French literature at the Sorbonne with Petit de Julleville between 1895 and 1897. Petit de Julleville's *Histoire du théâtre en France au moyen-âge* tells the story – which Synge summarized in Notebook 30 – of two men, one blind, one a cripple, who agree that the blind man will carry the cripple, each one thus compensating for the other's deficiency. When they are cured by a saint the cripple curses him because he has now lost the services of the blind man. In de Julleville's account the miracle was caused by a relic of St Martin, but Synge, drawing on memories of Irish holy wells and especially of one he had visited on the Aran Islands, has the Saint use holy water to effect cures. 'A couple of miles from this village we turned aside to look at an old ruined church of the Ceathair Aluinn (The Four Beautiful Persons), and a holy well near it that is famous for cures of blindness and epilepsy.' An old man told Synge that the well had become famous because its waters had cured a young child of its blindness.

Synge visited the well in the company of an old blind storyteller named Mourteen, and Mourteen's age, blindness and avid interest in sex may have influenced Synge in his characterization of Martin Doul. The face of old Mourteen 'was undescribably pliant, lighting up with an ecstasy of humour when he told me of anything that had a point of wit or malice, and growing sombre and desolate again when he spoke of religion or the fairies'. As he shows Synge an ancient, dimly lit beehive-dwelling he tells him 'what he would have done if he could have come in there when he was a young man and a young girl along with him'. When he points out the schoolmistress's house Mourteen exclaims, 'Wouldn't it be fine to be in there, and to be kissing her.'

The continual quarrelling between Martin and Mary Doul may have originated in Synge's memory of an Aran Island couple who quarrelled incessantly 'though they were as good friends as ever the next day'. Finally, the provenance of the play owes a great deal to a story Synge recorded in his article, 'The Vagrants of Wicklow', about an old man over ninety who was married again to a woman of eighty-five. On the honeymoon they quarrelled, he beat her with his stick, and set out alone again upon the roads. At her complaint he was arrested and had his fine white hair cut off in jail. Synge comments:

All his pride and his half-conscious feeling for the dignity of his age seemed to have set themselves on this long hair, which marked him out from the other people of this district; and I have often heard him saying to himself, as he sat beside me under a ditch: 'What use is an old man without his hair? A man has only his bloom like the trees; and what use is an old man without his white hair?'

It was from those varied incidents and acquaintances that Synge constructed the slight plot of *The Well of the Saints*. The cripple and the blind man of the original tale become the old blind beggars, Martin and Mary Doul. They live a relatively content life, having been persuaded by the villagers that they are a handsome couple. A holy man – 'A Wandering Friar' as he is called in the original Abbey Theatre programme – cures them of their blindness but now that they see how physically ugly they are, they quarrel and separate. They become blind again and are reconciled. When the holy man offers to cure them permanently, they refuse. Cherishing their illusions in preference to the starkness of reality, they set off on the dangerous roads to the south.

The original fifteenth-century source, *Moralité de l'aveugle et du boiteaux* by Andrieu de la Vigne, is clearly a farce, but there is little of the farcical in Synge's play. While there are moments of comedy, the mood of the play is closer to that of *King Lear* whose central metaphors also relate to seeing and blindness, and to illusion and reality. The movement and meaning of the play is reflected in the stage directions. The first act takes place at a crossroads in autumn. There is a wall 'with gap near centre' and the ruined doorway of a church. Quite clearly the crossroads and the ruined church represent that opposition between the tramp and the priest which is an enduring and obsessive theme in Synge's work. Act II, whose central dramatic action is the love scene between Martin and Molly, takes place in winter. The dominant images in this act are complemented by the props – broken wheels and a hell-like forge. In Act III the season is spring, and the stage directions indicate that the 'gap in centre' has been closed. But if the symbolism of spring and of the wheel come full circle seems to point to reconciliation, the final scene of the play subtly undercuts the possibility. In a dénouement that anticipates that of *The Playboy* we have a last glimpse of the blind old Martin Doul facing the mob 'defiantly' with a stone in his hand as his wife speaks in images of storm and death: 'and you going a stony path with a north wind blowing behind.' *(Plays* I, p. 151)

Synge's analysis of the play *(Plays* I, p. 264) makes it clear that he was primarily interested in the 'emotional subtlety' of his characters (Yeats's phrase). Act I probes the relationship of husband and wife. Act II, where Synge's writing is at its most sexual, dramatizes Martin Doul's lust for the physically beautiful. Act III dramatizes the compromises that life forces on its victims: the villagers enter the church to witness the marriage of Molly and the Smith – a marriage which clearly represents loss of freedom and creativity; the beggars escape to what is probably the illusory hope offered by Nature.

The opening scene of Act I, the exposition of 'character and psychics', is beautifully handled. When Martin and Mary first address each other, the 'psychics' of their relationships are immediately and effectively revealed. They quarrel and wrangle with each other, but they share a degree of good humour that prevents their altercations from developing into the naked cruelty that marks their exchanges following their cure.

Analysis Well of Saints

Act I	1. Martin and Mary	Exposition of characters and psychics
	2. + Timmy crescendo narrative	comedy
	3. + girls current more Martin excitement	
	4. + Saint	
	5. minus Saint	
	6. quarrel	tragic
Act II	Timmy and Martin no current	comic
	2. Martin and Molly Love current	traPoetical
Act III	Martin and Mary current of reawakened interest	
	2. plus crowd current to make Martin recured	

MARY DOUL: . . . Well, the sun's coming warm this day if it's late afternoon itself.

MARTIN DOUL: *(putting out his hands in sun)*. What way wouldn't it be warm and it getting high up in the south?

The 'psychics' of the scene are further developed as Martin, with unconscious irony, suggests that there is a puzzling disparity between Mary's beauty of person and harshness of voice:

MARTIN DOUL: *(teasingly, but with good-humour)*. I do be thinking odd times we don't know rightly what way you have your splendour, or asking myself, maybe, if you have it at all, for the time I was a young lad, and had fine sight, it was the ones with sweet voices were the best in face.

While developing the 'psychics' of the scene, Synge also develops his characters, stressing especially their differences. The keys to Mary's character are her vanity and her complacency. Mary, for example, turns Martin's charge that she has a 'queer cracked voice' to her advantage:

MARY DOUL: Who wouldn't have a cracked voice sitting out all the year in the rain falling? It's a bad life for the voice, Martin Doul, though I've heard tell there isn't anything like the wet south wind does be blowing upon us, for keeping a white beautiful skin – the like of my skin – on your neck and on your brows, and there isn't anything at all like a fine skin for putting splendour on a woman.

The key to Martin's character is his passionate nature and his strong sense of distinction. Lacking Mary's complacency his speeches are full of that ambivalence which is at the heart of the play:

> I do be thinking in the long nights it'd be a grand thing if we could see ourselves for one hour, or a minute itself, the way we'd know surely we were the finest man, and the finest woman, of the seven counties of the east . . . *(bitterly)* and then the seeing rabble below might be destroying their souls telling bad lies, and we'd never heed a thing they'd say.

As in the original medieval tale the blind man was forced to depend on the cripple for guidance, so Synge's beggars must depend on the lying rabble for assurances that they are handsome. The play then is about the blind leading the blind: Martin and Mary are physically blind and live contentedly enough in a world of illusion; the people of the village are sighted but figuratively they are blind and live wretchedly in the world of reality where they deliberately cultivate illusion. 'They're a bad lot those that have their sight,' Mary warns Martin, 'and they do have great joy, the time they do be seeing a grand thing, to let on they don't see it at all, and to be telling fools' lies.' *The Well of the Saints* dramatizes the beggars' journey from physical and spiritual blindness through sightedness, which Martin bitterly equates with the squalor of reality, to physical blindness again. In Act II, in the grotesque love scene between Martin and Molly, Synge intimates that the poet–lover can recreate the fallen world of reality and transform it into a higher world redeemed by imagination. But that intimation is undercut by the physical grossness of the lover and the spiritual grossness of the loved one. When Martin, now growing sightless again, learns the true nature of Molly, he joins in Mary's final, merciful self-deception. The only knowledge or wisdom that the beggars have learned in their bitter journey is that mutual self-deception is to be preferred to deception based on the lies of society. Disillusioned by the impossibility of ever attaining their dream, they choose blindness rather than reality.

It is part of Synge's purpose not to have us pity his beggars; to do so would be to weaken the intensity of those scenes where Martin and Mary are scourged by both physical and mental violence and cruelty. To achieve his purpose Synge makes both Martin and Mary creatures of violence and callousness. When Timmy the Smith tells them that a wonder will be done, the old couple try to guess what it is. Perhaps it will be a murder, Martin speculates, or the brewing of poteen – illegal whisky. Mary is even more brutal. 'Maybe they're hanging a thief, above at the bit of a tree? I'm told it's a great sight to see a man hanging by his neck, but what joy would that be to ourselves, and we not seeing it at all?' The macabre note sounded here is very like that in Beckett's *Waiting for Godot* where Estragon and Vladimir are attracted to the idea of committing suicide by hanging in order to get a final erection. Synge also anticipates Beckett in making his central characters truly repulsive. The 'wonder' that the holy man, or Saint, will perform will turn out to be the revelation to husband and wife of their mutual repulsiveness. 'The two of you will see a great wonder this day, and it's no lie,' Timmy says pityingly.

The entrance of the Saint in Act I is prefaced by the entrance of Molly and Bride who carry the Saint's bell, cloak and water-can containing the holy water. The play, to this point, has made it clear that Martin is powerfully attracted to the beautiful Molly. Molly, however, now conducts a mock trial of the blind man. She drapes him in the clothes and paraphernalia of the Saint, she and Bride mock him and strip him of the Saint's garments. The scene, like the final scene of *The Playboy,* parodies the incident in Christ's passion where He is dressed in a purple garment and mocked as a king. But Martin Doul is a Luciferian figure, not a Christ figure, as Synge is careful to point out. 'There's a grand handsome fellow, Mary Doul, and if you seen him now, you'd be as proud, I'm thinking, as the archangels below, fell out with the Almighty God.'

With the entrance of the Saint the opposition between beggar and priest is further developed. Unlike *The Tinker's Wedding* where old Mary is the too obvious mouthpiece of Synge's lesson, *The Well of the Saints* uses dramatic irony to undermine the seemingly sympathetic role played by the Saint. 'It's the like of you who are brave in a bad time will make a fine use of the gift of sight the Almighty God will bring to you to-day,' he declares, but in Act III Martin and Mary, recipients of God's 'gift', cower in a ditch for fear they will be discovered and irrevocably 'cured' of their physical blindness.

The scene in which Martin and Mary recover their sight and see each other for the first time is the most harrowing that Synge ever wrote, exceeded in intensity only by the concluding scene of Act II. When Martin returns from the church he finds Molly in Mary's usual place and presumes it is his wife. He cries out in ecstasy and adoration.

Oh, it was no lie they told me, Mary Doul. Oh, glory to God and the seven saints I didn't die and not see you at all. The blessing of God on the water, and the feet carried it round through the land. The blessing of God on this day, and them that brought me the saint, for it's grand hair you have *(she lowers her head, a little confused),* and soft skin, and eyes that would make the saints, if they were dark awhile and seeing again, fall down out of the sky. *(Plays* I, p. 95)

But he is rejected three times – by Molly, Bride and another village girl – and this scene where Martin stands baited by the villagers has affinities with Christy's trial scene in *The Playboy.*

The 'discovery' that follows, where Mary enters *'with a silly simpering smile',* has a two-fold function. In formal terms Synge is parodying the conventional 'discovery' scenes in comedy where hero and heroine surmount the difficulties that blocked their union and are united in a moment that clearly implies marriage. But Synge is also using the 'discovery' here to subvert normal values, values in this case associated with marriage. The ecstasy of Martin discovering Molly, the woman he lusts after, gives way to anguish and denunciation on discovering Mary, his wife. The animal imagery of their speeches amplifies the horror of the 'discovery':

MARTIN DOUL: *(breaking out into a passionate cry).* Your hair, and your big eyes, is it? . . . I'm telling you there isn't a wisp on any grey mare on the ridge of the world isn't finer than the dirty twist on your head. There isn't two eyes in any starving sow, isn't finer than the eyes you were calling blue like the sea.

MARY DOUL: *(interrupting him).* It's the devil cured you this day with your talking of sows; it's the devil cured you this day, I'm saying, and drove you crazy with lies.

In Synge's marriage of heaven and hell the Saint has now become a devil, his words lies, his gift of sight a curse. In the climactic speech of this scene Martin has a grotesque vision of people screaming for holy water that will bring blindness, not sight.

> MARTIN DOUL: Go on now to be seeking a lonesome place where the earth can hide you away, go on now, I'm saying, or you'll be having men and women with their knees bled, and they screaming to God for a holy water would darken their sight, for there's no man but would liefer be blind a hundred years, or a thousand itself, than to be looking on your like.

Synge's scenario called for the discovery scene between Martin and Mary to be tragic in character, but as husband and wife face each other murderously with raised sticks the scene is brutal and cruel, rather than tragic. 'The encounter upon the stage of two passionate manifestations, two living centers, two nervous magnetisms is something as entire, true, even decisive, as, in life, the encounter of one epidermis with another in a timeless debauchery,' wrote Artaud. 'That is why I propose a theater of cruelty.'[3]

In Act II the process of disillusionment is intensified. The hellish fires of the smith's forge, which symbolize Martin's lust for Molly, glow in a setting of winter, death and cruelty. 'I've heard tell you stripped the sheet from your wife and you putting her down into the grave,' Martin taunts Timmy, 'and that there isn't the like of you for plucking your living ducks, the short days, and leaving them running around in their skins, in the great rains and the cold.' Synge's scenario calls for the exchange between Martin and Timmy to be comic, but in the finished scene the comic has given way to the bitter:

J. M. Synge

MARTIN DOUL: *(very miserably)*. It's a hard thing for a man to have his sight, and he living near to the like of you *(he cuts a stick, and throws it away)*, or wed with a wife *(cuts a stick)*, and I do be thinking it should be a hard thing for the Almighty God to be looking on the world bad days, and on men the like of yourself walking around on it, and they slipping each way in the muck.

In Act I the villagers speak pityingly of the ugliness of the blind couple; in Act II, however, it is the sighted Martin and Mary who create confusion among the villagers by forcing them to look again at objects – reality – which formerly they had taken at face value. 'But it's a queer thing the way yourself and Mary Doul are after setting every person in this place, and up beyond Rathvanna talking of nothing, and thinking of nothing, but the way they do be looking in the face.' Synge is not as full-blown an idealist as Blake or Shelley, but in Act II of *The Well of the Saints* he does suggest strongly that reality is created by the imagination and is structured as we perceive it. In his poem, 'The Tower', Yeats writes of a 'country wench' whose beauty derives not from herself but from a poet who gave her her beauty. 'Farmers jostled at the fair / So great a glory did the song confer.' Synge will only partially accept this idea of the supremacy of the imagination (he distrusted the abstract), and in the love scene between Martin and Molly, where the dominating 'psychic' is sexuality, he will give it his characteristic twist by insisting that while Martin is, in some degree, a poet, he is, quite literally, a dirty old man.

Synge intended the love scene between Martin and Molly to act as ironic commentary on the discovery scene of Act I. The scene derives its effectiveness from the disproportion between the lovers in terms of age and beauty. This tryst at the well evokes echoes of the encounter in *Paradise Lost* between Eve and Satan ('Squat, like a toad, at the ear of Eve'), or that between Beauty and the Beast. Any attempt to sentimentalize, or refine, the Beast goes against Synge's intention. Joseph Holloway, who attended the première of *The Well of the Saints* and a revival of the play three years later, commented on the two Martins, revealing that the earlier characterization (which had Synge's approval) had been emasculated:

> The wild beast nature of 'Martin Doul' was artistically kept in check, and it made him a far more agreeable personage. W.G. Fay made him a very repulsive old man overwhelmed in sensuality. Arthur Sinclair made him more of a dreamer with a longing for the beautiful. . . . In fact, the play was lifted out of reality into the realm of fancy where it should have been from the first.[4]

Martin's attempted seduction of Molly is developed in a series of speeches that represent Synge's most explicit views on the nature and relationship of illusion and reality, the nature of love, and on the affinity between the peasant imagination and the artistic imagination which he had noted in *The Aran Islands*. The seduction begins on the sexual level as Martin says, *'with plaintive intensity'*, '. . . it's of many a fine thing your voice would put a poor dark fellow in mind, and the day I'd hear it, it's of little else at all I would be thinking.' Rebuked by Molly, Martin draws a contrast between the squalidness of reality and the glamour of illusion.

Grand day is it? *(Plaintively again, throwing aside his*

work, and leaning towards her.) Or a bad black day when I was roused up and found I was the like of the little children do be listening to the stories of an old woman, and do be dreaming after in the dark night that it's in grand houses of gold they are, with speckled horses to ride, and do be waking again, in a short while, and they destroyed with the cold, and the thatch dripping maybe, and the starved ass braying in the yard?

But Martin still retains one dream which is centred on Molly. 'For it's a fine sound your voice has that time, and it's better I am, I'm thinking, lying down, the way a blind man does be lying, than to be sitting here in the grey light, taking hard words of Timmy the smith.' The undercurrent of sexuality implied by the pun on 'lying' is caught and developed by Molly. 'And it's not his *lies* [Timmy's] you're making love to this day, Martin Doul'.

The tempter now offers Molly a vision of a life totally unlike that symbolized by the starved ass braying in the yard:

I've heard tell there are lands beyond in Cahir Iveraghig and the Reeks of Cork with warm sun in them, and fine light in the sky. *(Bending towards her.)* And light's a grand thing for a man ever was blind, or a woman, with a fine neck, and a skin on her like of you, the way we'd have a right to go off this day till we'd have a fine life passing abroad through them towns of the south, and we telling stories, maybe, or singing songs at the fairs.

It is a more optimistic vision than that offered Nora by the Tramp, and Synge adds a new dimension. Martin goes on to argue that only the blind have vision – 'it's few sees

104

anything but them is blind for a space.' The sighted, whose vision has been dimmed and coarsened by 'the contagion of the world's slow stain', see ugliness daily, the muck rather than the stars.

MARTIN DOUL: *(quickly, with low, furious intensity. He puts his hand on her shoulder and shakes her.)* You'd do right, I'm saying, not to marry a man is after looking out a long while on the bad days of the world, for what way would the like of him have fit eyes to look on yourself, when you rise up in the morning and come out of the little door you have above in the lane, the time it'd be a fine thing if a man would be seeing, and losing his sight, the way he'd have your two eyes facing him, and he going the roads, and shining above him, and he looking in the sky, and springing up from the earth, the time he'd lower his head, in place of the muck that seeing men do meet all roads spread on the world.

MOLLY BYRNE: *(who has listened, half-mesmerized, starting away).* It's the like of that talk you'd hear from a man would be losing his mind.

MARTIN DOUL: *(going after her, passing to her right).* It'd be little wonder if a man near the like of you would be losing his mind. Put down your can now, and come along with myself, for I'm seeing you this day, seeing you, maybe, the way no man has seen you in the world.

In this important exchange Synge comes closest in the play to equating the lust-driven, visionary Martin with the poet whose work, in Shelley's words, 'defeats the curse which binds us to be subjected to the accident of surrounding impressions. . . . it purges from our inward sight the film of familiarity which obscures from us the wonder of our being.'[5] Molly is drawn to the aged seducer because his words are in such marked contrast to her own cynicism. 'And what does any man care for a wife, when it's two weeks, or three, he is looking on her face?' she had asked earlier.

Synge's scenario called for the scene between Martin and Molly to be 'traPoetical', but again the climax of the scene is brutal rather than tragic, exceeding in its painfulness the climax of Act I. It is as harrowing as comparable moments in Shakespeare's bitter comedies – Malvolio's humiliation before his lady ('Madam, you have done me wrong / Notorious wrong'), or Shylock's debasement at the hands of his Christian baiters ('I pray you give me leave to go hence; / I am not well'). Martin, *'with imploring agony'*, beseeches Molly not to shame him by telling Mary what he has confided in her. As his blindness returns, his language becomes charged with apocalyptic imagery – the 'heavens are closing,' 'great trouble passing in the sky', 'darkness of thunder'; Mary strikes him across the face, and Molly mocks him. The scene, and the act, closes magnificently on Martin's curse where, in the most perverse gesture of the play, he prays that Molly and Timmy will be condemned to an eternity of loathsome copulation on a high bed in hell:

> Yet if I've no strength in me I've a voice left for my prayers, and may God blight them this day, and my own soul the same hour with them, the way I'll see them after, Molly Byrne and Timmy the smith, the two of them on a high bed, and they screeching in hell . . . . It'll be a grand thing that time to look on the two of them; and they twisting and roaring out, and twisting and roaring again, one day and the next day, and each day always and ever.

Act III operates at a much lower level of intensity than the other acts. It may be argued that this is a fault, that there is no 'rising line of interest to be followed with excitement', and that the language of the play 'swings to a rhythm that is too slow for drama'.[6] Yeats in his preface to the play saw these faults as virtues, as constituting the originality of Synge's art.

> It is the preoccupation of his characters with their dream that gives his plays their drifting movement, their emotional subtlety. . . . The ordinary student of drama will not find anywhere in *The Well of the Saints* that excitement of the will in the presence of attainable advantages, which he is accustomed to think the natural stuff of drama, and if he sees it played he will wonder why act is knitted to act so loosely, why it is all like a decoration on a flat surface, why there is so much leisure in the dialogue, even in the midst of passion.
>
> (*Plays* I, p. 67)

The first movement of the final act focuses on the reconciliation of Martin and Mary, on what Synge in his scenario terms the 'current of reawakened interest', and this is skilfully achieved by a number of subtle touches. The reconciliation had already been prepared for by various 'hooks' in Act II: Mary's unwillingness to abandon her husband – 'Well, isn't it a queer thing she can't keep herself two days without looking on my face?' – and her claim that Molly's beauty is the kind that will fade quickly – 'It's them that's fat and flabby do be wrinkled young, and that whitish yellowy hair she has does be soon turning the like of a handful of thin grass you'd see rotting, where the wet lies, at the north of a sty.' Martin's opening speech in Act III, in which he expresses his profound loneliness, allows Synge to effect a reconciliation in keeping with the

violent and unsentimental nature of man and wife. 'It's
lonesome I'll be from this day, and if living people is a bad
lot, yet Mary Doul herself, and she a dirty, wrinkled-
looking hag, was better maybe to be sitting along with
than nobody at all.' Mary, developing her remarks about
her superiority to Molly, lays claim to a unique beauty –
the whiteness of her hair. In a further ironic inversion, she
claims to have seen her beauty reflected in a well. The title
of the play can now be seen to be richly ambiguous for the
Saints of the well may, in reality, be Martin and Mary.
Martin, seeking to match Mary's claim (which can be
interpreted either as an act of imagination or as an escape
into the world of illusion), hits on the idea of growing a
beard. In a marvellous turnabout they make a virtue of
old age, finding a beauty in mortality as they have come to
find vision in blindness: 'I've this to say, Mary Doul, I'll
be letting my beard grow in a short while – a beautiful,
long, white, silken, streamy beard, you wouldn't see the
like of in the eastern world . . . . Ah, a white beard's a
grand thing on an old man.'

The harmony now established between the two beggars
is beautifully symbolized in two speeches extolling the
return of spring and birth:

MARY DOUL: There's the sound of one of them twittering
yellow birds do be coming in the spring-time from
beyond the sea, and there'll be a fine warmth now in
the sun, and a sweetness in the air, the way it'll be a
grand thing to be sitting here quiet and easy, smelling
the things growing up, and budding from the earth.

MARTIN DOUL: I'm smelling the furze a while back
spouting on the hill, and if you'd hold your tongue
you'd hear the lambs of Grianan, though it's near
drowned their crying is with the full river making
noises in the glen.

It is at this moment, when the two old people have become reconciled, that the Saint's bell is heard. It is an ominous sound, totally at variance with the music of nature. It is a measure of Synge's art that all our sympathies are with the old beggars as they seek desperately to hide from the Saint, and the girls, like Molly, with 'sharp terrible eyes'. There is a profound pathos when Mary, 'nearly in tears', cries out, '. . . what good'll our grey hairs be itself, if we have our sight, the way we'll see them falling each day, and turning dirty in the rain?' The poignancy of the speech derives from Mary's recognition that they have deliberately given themselves over to illusion.

The 'psychics' of the remainder of Act III turn on the conflict or debate between the tinker and the Saint. It is a restatement of the conflict between the tinker and the Priest in *The Tinker's Wedding,* but this restatement is far subtler. It is given dramatic tension because the Saint makes it clear that those he cures a second time 'go on seeing till the hour of death'. The Saint begins the debate by claiming that people are beautiful because they are created in God's image: Martin retorts that when he was given sight he saw how truly ugly people were. The Saint praises nature because it has been sanctified by the churches built throughout the land by holy men; Martin's retort carries Synge's belief that nature in itself is hostile and needs internalization in the imagination to become fruitful:

Isn't it finer sights ourselves had a while since and we sitting dark smelling the sweet beautiful smells do be rising in the warm nights and hearing the swift flying things racing in the air (SAINT *draws back from him),* till we'd be looking up in our minds into a grand sky, and seeing lakes, and broadening rivers, and hills waiting

109

for the spade and plough.   (*Plays* I, p. 141)

When Martin strikes the tin can holding the holy water from the Saint's hand, the plausibility of the action is typical of Synge's dramatic method in rooting complex ideas in physical detail. He rejects the Saint's cure in language that clearly shows he is also rejecting the Saint's asceticism which is seen to be unnatural. 'Let you walk on now with your worn feet, and your welted knees, and your fasting, holy ways have left you with a big head on you and a thin pitiful arm.'

In the final scene of the play the beggars are stoned by the people and driven away, as Nora Burke was driven away by her husband. As Martin Doul stands, stone in hand, facing the hostile mob, the scene also anticipates the torturing of Christy Mahon in *The Playboy* and his final defiance of the jeering villagers. The close of *The Well of the Saints* also resembles that of *The Shadow of the Glen* in its melancholy and premonitory sense of death. Martin is more optimistic than Mary about travelling south to a new and unknown country but he uses the word 'maybe' to qualify his hopes. 'For we're going on the two of us to the towns of the south, where the people will have kind voices maybe, and we won't know their bad looks or their villainy at all.' Mary's final speech is marked by the same stoicism which marked the final speeches of Nora Burke and Maurya. 'That's the truth, surely, and we'd have a right to be gone, if it's a long way itself, where you do have to be walking with a slough of wet on the one side and a slough of wet on the other, and you going a stony path with a north wind blowing behind.' It's a bitter vision, prophetic perhaps of their destruction ('I'm thinking the two of them will be drowned,' Timmy remarks callously), but Synge has clearly intimated that in questing southwards they have chosen more wisely than the villagers who pass through the ruined doorway of the church to witness the wedding of Molly to the 'almost elderly' smith.

'The harder the struggle for life and the more one's weakness is felt, the greater becomes the need for mutual deception,' Pirandello writes. 'The "humorist" at once picks out such various simulations, amuses himself by unmasking them; is not indignant about them – he simply is that way.'[7] What is remarkable about *The Well of the Saints* is Synge's willingness to abide in uncertainties, and his ability to dramatize the possibility that illusion may be superior to reality, and that self-deception in pursuit of the dream is permissible, even praiseworthy.

The Well of the Saints is also a magnificent affirmation of the ego's need to be recognized as distinctive, if not unique. The earlier plays had been haunted by Synge's sense of mortality, but in this play so rich and abundant are the two beggars that they transform the very symbol of age and death – white hair – into that which guarantees these two outcasts their distinction and their uniqueness. Finally, it should be noted that the agent of this transformation is imagination as expressed through language. Synge's genius is manifest in his ability to take a complex and literary theme – the power of the imagination to transform reality – and make of it a work of art instilled with drama and theatricality.

7
'The Playboy of the Western World'

The Playboy of the Western World is Synge's masterpiece, the play which brought him international fame. By having Christy Mahon, the Playboy, believe mistakenly that he has killed his father, Synge explores the comic possibilities of the Oedipal theme which involves both parricide and incest. This brilliant and extravagant comedy is given tragic overtones as Synge once again contrasts the world of dream or illusion (the Playboy's world) with the world of gross reality unredeemed by the imagination (the peasant's world). When the play was first presented at the Abbey Theatre, Dublin audiences rioted, affronted by the violence of the action and by the image of Ireland which it embodied.

Between 1903 and 1905 Synge made a number of visits to West Kerry and to the wild and poverty-stricken Congested Districts of Mayo which he described in various articles published in *The Shanachie* and the *Manchester Guardian*. While these articles are inferior to those which make up *The Aran Islands* (Yeats felt they should not be

112

published), they are important in that they provide us with the provenance of *The Playboy of the Western World*. Notebook 52, for example, which contains eighteen pages of notes on County Mayo, and analyses of the drama of Racine and Molière, contains early sketches for *The Playboy*. The hills and glens of Wicklow could not compare in grandeur and wildness with the landscape of Kerry and North Mayo and whereas in the Wicklow plays Synge had been primarily concerned with the psychology of the peasant and the tinker, the physical violence and extravagance of speech and action which he noted in Kerry and Mayo found expression in *The Playboy*. In Kerry, for example, Synge saw how the girls sat stroking the arms and face of a young man, thrown from a cart, whose face was 'still raw and bleeding and horrible to look at' as if they found romance in his condition. He heard stories of the drowning of a 'mergency man (an officer who assists with evictions), and of a mermaid married to a mortal who later returned to the sea and enticed her own children to their deaths. He learned why a sandy head of land was called the Stooks of the Dead Women: 'for one time a boat came ashore there with twelve dead women on board her, big ladies with green dresses and gold rings, and fine jewelries, and a dead harper or fiddler along with them,' *(Prose,* p. 264) and he transposed the memorably named spot from Kerry to the Mayo of *The Playboy:* 'It's a queer daughter you are if you'd have me crossing backward through the Stooks of the Dead Women, with a drop taken,' Michael James complains to his daughter, Pegeen Mike. Synge also watched races on the strand near the Kerry town of Dingle and later he learned what happened when the men got drunk:

'There was great sport after you left,' a man said to me

J. M. Synge

in the cottage this evening. 'They were all beating and
cutting each other on the shore of the sea. Four men
fought together in one place till the tide came up on
them, and was like to drown them; but the priest waded
out up to his middle and drove them asunder. Another
man was left for dead on the road outside the lodges,
and some gentleman found him and had him carried
into his house, and got the doctor to put plasters on his
head. Then there was a red-headed fellow had his finger
bitten through, and the postman was destroyed forever.'   *(Prose, p. 275)*

The West of Ireland, particularly Mayo, reinforced
Synge's attraction to the violence and lawlessness of the
Irish peasant. Mayo had always been an area of great
poverty and violence. Boycotting was widely practised
and it was in Mayo that Synge's brother, Edward, evicted
'a whole townland' of peasants. A particularly cruel aspect
of the agrarian wars was the maiming by the peasants of
the landlords' cattle and sheep as a retaliatory measure. In
The Playboy Marcus Quinn, who has a great warrant to
tell stories of holy Ireland, got 'six months for maiming
ewes'.

Synge was also appalled by the poverty he saw in Mayo
and by the damage it did the people. 'In Mayo,' he writes,
'one cannot forget that in spite of the beauty of the
scenery the people in it are debased and nearly demoral-
ized by bad housing and the endless misery of the rain.'
(Prose, p.316, n. 1) On his return in 1905 from a visit to
Mayo, Synge wrote to his friend, Stephen MacKenna:

There are sides of all that western life, the groggy-
patriot – publican – general-shop-man who is married to
the priest's half sister and is second cousin once-

removed of the dispensary doctor, that are horrible and awful. This is the type that is running the present United Irish League anti-grazier campaign, while they're swindling the people themselves in a dozen ways and then buying out their holdings and packing off whole families to America. . . . I sometimes wish to God I hadn't a soul and then I could give myself up to putting those lads on the stage. God, wouldn't they hop!   *(Prose,*p. 283n)

It was against this background of wilderness, poverty, violence, degeneracy and lawlessness (so different from the idealized nobility of the Aran peasantry in *Riders to the Sea)* that Synge began working on his 'extravagant comedy' which was variously called 'The Murderer (A Farce)', 'Murder Will Out, or the Fool of the Family', and 'The Fool of Farnham', until he hit upon the final, splendidly ambiguous title, *The Playboy of the Western World.*

In his programme notes for the 26 January 1907 premi-ère of the play Synge stressed that he had used 'very few words that I have not heard among the country people' and further claimed that 'the same is true also, to some extent, of the actions and incidents I work with. The central incident of the Playboy was suggested by an actual occurrence in the West.' When the play was published Synge, stung by criticism that the play was a libel upon the Irish, wrote in the preface to the play that the 'wildest sayings and ideas' in it were tame compared to the fancies he was accustomed to hear in the countryside. This is a much stronger claim than that advanced in the programme notes. But if we compare the account Synge recorded in *The Aran Islands* with his version in *The Playboy* one can easily see that it is the Aran account which pales in comparison with Synge's wild, extravagant and morally nihilistic recreation of it.

In *The Aran Islands* account a Connaught man who had killed his father in a fit of passion is sheltered from the police until he can finally escape to America. Synge, commenting on the psychology of the story, writes that 'this impulse to protect the criminal is universal in the west' because of 'the association between justice and the hated English jurisdiction'. These primitive people will only commit a crime, he goes on, when 'under the influence of a passion which is as irresponsible as a storm on the sea'. *(Prose,* p. 95) The third point, Synge notes admiringly, is that the islanders remained 'incorruptible' in spite of a reward which was offered.

Synge's changes and innovations in handling this story are radical and characteristic. In the Aran account the parricide is excused, in *The Playboy* it is glorified. With his eye directly on his Sophoclean model, Synge celebrates what had been traditionally regarded as the most heinous of crimes – the killing of a parent. When Oedipus discovered that he had unknowingly killed his father and married his mother, he gouged out his eyeballs with Jocasta's golden brooches and willingly accepted banishment from his kingdom. Christy Mahon knowingly kills his father but is rewarded by the approval of the villagers, the admiration of the local girls and the courtship of two fine women who seek him in marriage. Here Synge introduced a new motif totally lacking in the Aran account but present in his Sophoclean model – incest. Through many drafts of *The Playboy* Synge toyed with the idea of having the Playboy marry the Widow Quin, clearly a surrogate for the Widow Casey who suckled him for six weeks. In one account the Playboy claims he killed his father because he was being forced by him to marry this mother figure. (*Plays* II, p. 101)

Another radical difference is also important in showing how Synge changed the Aran account. There the islanders are innocent and idealized, proof in their loyalties against the reward offered an informer. But in *The Playboy* the men are degenerate and lawless, and Pegeen Mike – a far cry from Mangan's Dark Rosaleen or Yeats's Cathleen Ni Houlihan – leads them in betraying their father-killer and handing him over to the hated English jurisdiction. Bourgeois, commenting on the play, claims that it is 'Irish in view of its being an extremely searching study of the Celtic temperament, with its ever-possible imaginative perversion of ethical ideals'.[1]

Interpretations of *The Playboy of the Western World* are many and varied. It has been viewed as an allegory of Synge's own growth as an artist; as a parody of *Oedipus Rex;* as a parody of Christ's ministry and crucifixion; as a satire on Irish blarney and love of a tall tale well told; as a prime example of metatheatre (the characters are aware of their own theatricality, and illusion seems more real than reality); as a successful translation of dream into reality.[2] Like all masterpieces *The Playboy* is susceptible of many interpretations.

The action of the play takes place in a public house – and it is framed by an imminent wedding and a wake. The naturalism of the interior is balanced by a sense of the outside world ('on a wild coast of Mayo') as a landscape of nightmare and menace. It is a time of 'broken harvests and the ended wars'; the countryside is threatened by 'harvest boys with their tongues red for drink' and 'loosèd khaki cut-throats' and the 'walking dead'.

The inhabitants of the nearby villages (appropriately named Killamuck and Killakeen) are a degenerate, lawless and cruel breed. They include the squint-eyed Red

Linahan, the lame Patcheen, the mad Mulrannies, Daneen Sullivan who blinded a policeman, Marcus Quin who mutilated ewes, the Widow Quin who murdered her husband and suckled a ram at her breast, boys who stoned a madman 'till he ran out raving and foaming and was drowned in the sea'. Shawn Keogh, Pegeen's future husband, is a cowardly, treacherous, priest-ridden farmer, a degenerate Michael Dara, one of the 'ungodly ruck of fat-faced, sweaty-headed swine' Synge described in a letter to Stephen MacKenna. *(Prose,* p. 283n) The 'fat and amorous' Jimmy Farrell spent three hours hanging his dog and Sarah Tansey, one of the village girls, once drove ten miles to see 'the man bit the yellow lady's nostril'.

At first glance, Pegeen Mike may seem an exception to the people who surround her. She is one of Synge's finest creations, a challenge to any young actress. Influenced too heavily by Christy's love speeches extolling her beauty and wonder, too many actresses err in giving her a glamour and beauty she possesses only for the Playboy. His praise is undercut by the Widow Quin's description: 'a girl you'd see itching and scratching, and she with a stale stink of poteen on her from selling in the shop'. If Pegeen is glamorized or if Christy is cast as a romantic lead, the play will lack that brutality which Synge felt was a necessary element of the poetic. The actress, Marie Nic Shiubhlaigh, writing in 1956, noted this tendency to 'sanitize' *The Playboy.* 'Produced nowadays, the play is done as a comedy – and is invariably successful. When it was given for the first time it was played seriously, almost sombrely, as though each character had been studied and its nastiness made apparent.'[3]

There is a suggestion in the opening scene of the play that Pegeen has something of Nora Burke's melancholy. As she winds the clock she says, 'Isn't it long nights are now, Shawn Keogh, to be leaving a poor girl with her own self counting the hours to the dawn of day?' But it is a suggestion that is not developed in the play. Nora, in keeping with the quieter and more psychologically oriented mood of *The Shadow of the Glen,* is haunted by a sense of time and mortality; Pegeen, within the more physical context of *The Playboy,* has no such sense, fearing only physical danger. This despite the fact that she is a virago, feared by all. Jimmy Farrell calls her 'a fine, hardy girl would knock the head of any two men in the place', and Shawn says she has 'the devil's own temper'. Pegeen herself admits to being 'the fright of seven townlands' because of her biting tongue. Like Katharina in *The Taming of the Shrew,* she is given to violence, and this predominant aspect of her nature is expressed in images of brutality and torture that recur in many of her speeches. When it is her turn to question Christy Mahon about his crime, she asks: 'You never hanged him, the way Jimmy Farrell hanged his dog from the licence and had it screeching and wiggling three hours at the butt of a string?' Jealous of the village girls, she frightens Christy with a description of the burial of a hanged criminal: 'When it's dead he is, they'd put him in a narrow grave, with cheap sacking wrapping him round, and pour down quicklime on his head, the way you'd see a woman pouring any frish-frash from a cup.' Significantly, she returns to Farrell's hanging his dog further to terrify Christy: 'it'd make the green stones cry itself to think of you swaying and swiggling at the butt of a rope.' It is entirely in character that Pegeen would hand Christy over to the law – 'or the lot of us will be likely put on trial for his deed to-day' – and that she should be the one to torture him by burning. There is, then, a profound and comic irony in Christy's remark as he first surveys the shebeen and its inhabitants: 'It's a safe house, so.'

Christy's first exchange with the villagers is an important one for it tells us a great deal about his character and about how Synge means us to gauge his irony. Critics, anxious to emphasize Christy's development in the play, tend to underestimate his native shrewdness and instinct for survival. The villagers engage with Christy in a grotesque flyting or *iomarbháigh* in which they try to guess what crime he has committed. The Gaelic term, *iomarbháigh,* has two meanings implying both a contest and a boastful dispute.[4] In this contest the villagers run through a catalogue of possible crimes (a parody of the epic hero's deeds) – larceny, rape, murder. Christy scorns these crimes as being merely 'stories on any little paper of a Munster town'. The villagers, *'with delighted curiosity',* return to the contest guessing the crime to be forgery, bigamy, treason. But with his confession that his crime is parricide Christy emerges as clear winner in the contest of wits as he will later emerge victor in the contests on the strand. The exchange continues as the villagers now attempt to determine what weapon was used – pistol, knife or rope. Again Christy outwits them – it was a loy, prosaic version of the epic hero's sword or spear. Christy is clearly a *miles gloriosus* whose braggadocio out-rivals that of his opponents and whose actions parody those of an epic hero. Following Christy's victory Synge effects a marvellous marriage of the naturalistic and the grotesque. Pegeen is afraid of spending the night alone; Shawn is afraid to stay with her lest he incur the wrath of Fr Reilly; Michael James wants to get away to Kate Cassidy's wake where he can drink all night. Christy provides the perfect resolution; he is a comic *deus ex machina* whose acceptance as pot-boy (his reward for winning the contest of wits) answers all these difficulties. 'Now, by the grace of

God, herself will be safe this night,' Jimmy Farrell declares, 'with a man killed his father holding danger from the door, and let you come on, Michael James, or they'll have the best stuff drunk at the wake.' The solution may be grotesque but within this lawless Mayo society it has its own compelling logic; the entire scene is a classic example of Synge's penchant for turning values upside down. The parricide, by common consent, is best qualified to protect the virtue of this Irish Dulcinea after he is judged by Jimmy to be brave, by Pegeen to be wise, and by Philly to be such a terror to the police that they would stay away from the shebeen where illegal whisky is often sold. In as vivid a phrase as Synge ever coined Philly remarks, 'There isn't one of them would come smelling around if the dogs itself were lapping poteen from the dung-pit of the yard.'

To strengthen further the appropriateness in having Christy as Pegeen's protector, Synge employs Shawn as the mouthpiece of conventional values and of the apprehensions an audience might feel. 'That'd be a queer kind to bring into a decent quiet household with the like of Pegeen Mike.' But because Synge has already undermined Shawn as a moral gauge the audience is forced to side with Pegeen and Michael James against Shawn as it was manipulated by Synge to side with the tinkers against the Priest in *The Tinker's Wedding* and with Martin and Mary Doul against the Saint. Synge, like William Blake, is clearly on the side of the Devils. In *The Marriage of Heaven and Hell* one proverb reads, 'If the fool would persist in his folly he would become wise.' Christy, having been accepted as pot-boy, will now pursue his folly and achieve as ambiguous a wisdom as Don Quixote or Molière's Alceste.

In the scene between Pegeen and Christy which follows the departure of the other men, the sub-current is the 'growing love interest'. The main current is clearly the counterpointing of Pegeen's romanticized view of Christy with his own prosaic account of his life before he killed his father. Pegeen, watching Christy *'with delight'*, calls him 'a fine, handsome young fellow with a noble brow', a poet like Owen Roe O'Sullivan, 'the like of a King of Norway or the Eastern World'. But Christy, in Act I, consistently opposes his realistic view of himself to what he considers is Pegeen's false view of him. 'The like of a King, is it! And I after toiling, moiling, digging, dodging from the dawn till dusk with never a sight of joy or sport saving only when I'd be abroad in the dark night poaching rabbits on hills.' Seduced, however, by the admiration of the villagers Christy will begin to fashion himself in Act II as a hero matching their illusions.

When Christy is first spoken of in the play before his appearance, he is described as a fellow 'above in the furzy ditch, groaning wicked like a maddening dog' in a 'dark lonesome place'. This is an early suggestion that he is like the Tramp in *The Shadow of the Glen* who comes into the house from a dark, stormy night; the imagery harks back also to Patch Darcy who went mad and died in the ditch. Christy, like the Tramp and Patch Darcy, is a solitary man and it is precisely this solitude which Pegeen fears and does not understand. 'And it's that you'd call sport is it, to be abroad in the darkness with yourself alone?' The play draws a clear opposition between the shebeen and nature; the shebeen is no more a safe house than was Dan Burke's. Some critics feel that Christy's poetry in wooing Pegeen and his prowess in winning the games on the strand symbolize his growth to maturity. On the contrary, they symbolize his progressively dangerous identification with the corrupt world of the villagers. Christy, like Nora Burke, must be rejected by the debased society he embraces so enthusiastically in order that he may seek the lonely and difficult freedom of men like the Tramp, Patch Darcy and Martin Doul.

In his discussion of what he terms the third phase of comedy, where 'a *senex iratus* or other humor gives way to a young man's desires,' Northrop Frye writes: 'The presiding genius of comedy is Eros, and Eros has to adapt himself to the moral facts of society: Oedipus and incest themes indicate that erotic attachments have in their undisplaced or mythical origin a much greater versatility.'[5] Because Synge considered Mayo to be a lawless place, little touched by 'the moral facts of society', he could allow Eros a versatility that embraces both parricide and incest. The Widow Quin is an Irish Jocasta, a cynical mother–whore figure, who challenges Pegeen for Christy. In Act I Christy tells Pegeen, 'We're alike so', but as the play develops Synge draws a number of correspondences between Christy and the widow. Both are murderers – her 'sneaky kind of murder' resembles Christy's 'dirty deed'; both are outsiders – 'You'll be doing like myself, I'm thinking, when I did destroy my man,' the Widow Quin says, '. . . and myself living alone.' 'You're like me, so,' Christy declares and the Widow agrees. 'I am your like.' Pegeen triumphs over the Widow in the closing scene of Act I, but her final speech in that act suggests that the triumph is not a final one and that Christy may be forced to turn to the Widow Quin for help. 'May God give you a good rest till I call you in the morning when the cocks will crow,' Pegeen says. Within the amoral world of Christy Mahon the cock symbolizes rebirth; within the repressive, nominally Christian world of Mayo the cock signifies betrayal.

'Act II has far too much padding in it,' Professor Corkery has complained. 'The only essential point in it is the entrance of the Playboy's father.' Act II involves some repetition – Christy's retelling of how he killed his father and another love scene with Pegeen – but if we understand that Synge is moving from the naturalism that generally pervades Act I to the extravaganza that dominates Act II we can see how such scenes enrich the play's theme and further its design. For example, Christy's retelling of the parricide in Act II, when contrasted with the bare, prosaic account in Act I, shows his development as mock hero and poet–braggart. 'He gave a drive with the scythe, and I gave a lep to the east. Then I turned around with my back to the north, and I hit a blow on the ridge of his skull, laid him stretched out, and he split to the knob of his gullet.' This is a fight of titans who straddle the earth, reaching all points of the compass; typically, its heroic proportions are undercut by Christy's weapons – a tea mug and a chicken bone.

The same mock glorification is at work in the opening scene of Act II where Christy receives homage and presents from the local girls. This scene is a parody of the Epiphany and the Magi's presentation of gifts to the Christ–child.[6] It is also rich with echoes of the story of the three Marys who sought out Christ at the tomb after His crucifixion and found the linen which signified that He was risen. Synge's three girls come running over the fields to the shebeen to see the new hero and find no one there. Says Honor, 'He's been sleeping there in the night. Well, it'll be a hard case if he's gone off now.' The business with Christy's boots is a comic allusion to the linen found in Christ's tomb. After the presentation of the pullet, Sarah asks, 'Is your right hand too sacred for to use at all?' Synge said of this scene, '. . . it's extravagant, it's extravagance (how's it spelt?). So is *Don Quixote*.'[7]

The second scene between Christy and Pegeen differs

from that of Act I in that it is less a love scene than a dialogue on the nature of solitude. In Act I Pegeen had expressed puzzlement – disbelief even – at the Playboy's delight 'to be abroad in the darkness with [himself] alone'. She returns now to the same theme:

> PEGEEN: I'm thinking you're an odd man, Christy Mahon. The oddest walking fellow I ever set my eyes on to this hour to-day.
> CHRISTY: What would any be but odd men and they living lonesome in the world?
> PEGEEN: I'm not odd, and I'm my whole life with my father only.

An early 'Murder Will Out' draft of these lines provides a gloss on the meaning of the important word 'odd' which occurs so frequently in Synge's plays:

> PEGEEN: You're talking as if you were after being a tramp from your birth, when you said last night it was a week only since you'd quit the place where you were reared.
> CHRISTY: I'll be a tramp I'm thinking from this day to my death and hasn't a man a right to look before him, when he's sickened with looking behind?

The dialogue continues in *The Playboy:*

> PEGEEN: Would you have me think a man never talked with the girls would have the words you've spoken to-day? It's only letting on you are to be lonesome, the way you'd get around me now.
> CHRISTY: I wish to God I was letting on; but I was lonesome all times and born lonesome, I'm thinking,

125

as the moon of dawn. *(Going to door.)*

PEGEEN: *(puzzled by his talk).* Well, it's a story I'm not understanding at all why you'd be worse than another, Christy Mahon, and you a fine lad with the great savagery to destroy your da.

This is a seminal exchange which anticipates Pegeen's ultimate rejection of the Playboy. He is a solitary, a tramp; the parricide represents a necessary rejection of all symbols of kinship and authority – family, priest, society. The consequences, if liberating, are terrifying, for humankind cannot bear too much solitude. The Tramp of *The Shadow of the Glen* may go mad like Patch Darcy; the Playboy, as he intimates in the torture scene of Act III, may end up 'like the madmen of Keel, eating muck and green weeds on the faces of the cliffs'. Synge's work deals with the theme of dream versus reality, but even more important is the theme of human liberty and how it can only be achieved – and retained – through the rejection of all conventional authority. In one of the funniest speeches of the play, even Shawn recognizes this. 'Oh, it's a hard case to be a orphan and not to have your father that you're used to, and you'd easy kill and make yourself a hero in the sight of all.' But Shaw has a father – Father Reilly – who represents that institutionalized religion which Synge believed restricted human liberty and creativity.

The entrance of Old Mahon rings further changes on the theme of role-playing. Christy, in Act I, had presented his father as a phallic and mythic figure: 'and he after drinking for weeks, rising up in the red dawn, or before it maybe, and going out into the yard as naked as an ash tree in the moon of May, and shying clods again the visage of the stars.' This picture is reinforced in Act II in Christy's description of their epic battle. But when the Widow Quin first sees Old Mahon she exclaims in surprise, 'Is it that tramper?' We are forced to balance Christy's picture of him as a godlike figure of virility and authority against the widow's – her attitude to Old Mahon is one of amusement – just as we are forced to balance the villagers' impression of Christy against that of Old Mahon's. His father pictures Christy as someone shy of women, unmanly ('I had to send him in the cart to the female nurse'), narcissistic ('making mugs at his own self in the bit of a glass we had hung on the wall'), a fool ('the looney of Mahon's'). Paradoxically, Synge makes a further daring equation: in the mirror of the Widow Quin's amused irony father and son seem alike:

> WIDOW QUIN: I'd give the world and all to see the like of him. What kind was he?
> MAHON: A small low fellow.
> WIDOW QUIN: And dark?
> MAHON: Dark and dirty.
> WIDOW QUIN: *(considering)*. I'm thinking I seen him.
> MAHON: *(eagerly)*. An ugly young blackguard.
> WIDOW QUIN: A hideous, fearful villain, and the spit of you.

Some critics have faulted the conclusion of Act II. The drafts of the final scene lend support to these charges; the Widow's final speech gave Synge great trouble. His difficulty arose from the fact that, having introduced Old Mahon in Act II, he seems not to know what to do with him until the dénouement of Act III. It would have been dramatically more effective to have delayed Old Mahon's entrance until Act III. The Widow Quin's stratagem – 'We'll swear he's a maniac and not your da' *(Plays* II,p. 131) – is too pat a solution to Christy's fear his father will return. Even Philly sees its transparency. 'You're at some gaming, Widow Quin; but I'll walk after him and give him his dinner and a time to rest, and I'll see then if he's raving or as sane as you.'

The third act opens on a wonderfully macabre note that would have delighted Jacobean dramatists. Philly O'Cullen drunkenly converses with Jimmy Farrell on graveyards and skulls. 'When I was a young lad,' says Philly,

> there was a graveyard beyond the house with the remnants of a man who had thighs as long as your arm. He was a horrid man, I'm telling you, and there was many a fine Sunday I'd put him together for fun, and he with shiny bones you wouldn't meet the like of these days in the cities of the world.

The naturalism of Act I and the extravaganza of Act II give way in Act III to the grotesque and the surreal; the dissonance set up by the counterpoint of tragedy and comedy, horror and laughter, becomes almost too disturbing. It was late in Act III that the first Dublin audience rioted, enraged (among other considerations) by the accumulated savagery of imagery, characterization and action. 'I knew a party was kicked in the head by a red mare, and he went killing horses a great while, till he eat the insides of a clock and died after,' says Jimmy. Old Mahon, convinced by the Widow Quin that he is mad, finds distinction in his lunacy. 'There was one time I seen ten scarlet divils letting on they'd cork my spirit in a gallon can; and one time I seen rats as big as badgers sucking the life blood from the butt of my lug.' A drunken Michael James describes Kate Cassidy's wake: 'you'd never see the match of it for flows of drink, the way when we sunk her bones at noonday in her narrow grave, there were five men, aye and six men, stretched out retching speechless on the holy stones.'

The famous love scene of Act III contains some of Synge's finest writing. The entire language of *The Playboy* is rich and functional, every speech 'as fully flavoured as a nut or apple'. But in this final love scene Synge combined the richness of colloquial West Ireland dialect with an even more heightened use of rhythm, cadence and metaphor to create the most rapturous love duet of modern drama. Only in opera, in such love duets as those in *Tristan and Isolde ('O sink hernieder, Nacht der Liebe'),* or *Otello ('Già nella notte densa'),* do we find the same sense of ecstasy intensified by motifs which intimate that it will be succeeded by pain, betrayal or death:

> CHRISTY: *(with rapture).* If the mitred bishops seen you that time, they'd be the like of the holy prophets, I'm thinking, do be straining the bars of Paradise to lay eyes on the Lady Helen of Troy, and she abroad pacing back and forward with a nosegay in her golden shawl.

Synge tried more than a dozen versions of this speech before he got the effect he wanted; the final collocation of the sacred and the profane, the heroic and the mythic, transforms Margaret Flaherty temporarily into as potent a symbol as Helen of Troy.

Many critics feel that this final love scene signifies the full flowering of Christy as hero and poet. 'He actually possesses those qualities which Pegeen and the others fancied they saw in him at first,' writes Dr Price.[8] But if Synge has already given us enough hints to see that Pegeen is, by nature, unfitted to match the vision which Christy offers her, then the scene should be read bearing in mind that Synge is here counterpointing the satiric and the lyrical as he had continually counterpointed the satiric and the epic in the first two acts. To read the love scene without reference to Synge's enduring irony is like reading the love scenes of *Troilus and Cressida* in ignorance of Thersites's warning, 'All the argument is a cuckold and a whore.'

> PEGEEN: *(with real tenderness)*. And what is it I have, Christy Mahon, to make me fitting entertainment for the like of you have such poet's talking, and such bravery of heart?
>
> CHRISTY: *(in a low voice)*. Isn't there the light of seven heavens in your heart alone, the way you'll be an angel's lamp to me from this out, and I abroad in the darkness spearing salmons in the Owen or Carrowmore.
>
> PEGEEN: If I was your wife, I'd be along with you those nights, Christy Mahon, the way you'd see I was a great hand at coaxing bailiffs, or coining funny nicknames for the stars of night.
>
> CHRISTY: You, is it! Taking your death in the hailstones or the fogs of dawn.

'And I abroad in the darkness . . .' Even in his most impassioned declaration of love Christy emphasizes his delight in a solitude Pegeen does not really understand. When Pegeen's father gives his blessing to the lovers in a scene that prefigures their marriage, he comments on the solitary state which the Playboy has now escaped. 'What's a single man, I ask you, eating a bit in one house and drinking a sup in another, and he with no place of his own, like an old braying jackass strayed upon the rocks?'

The pattern of comedy, to this point in the play, seems

fairly clear. A love relationship that has been blocked by opposition – Shawn's and Pegeen's father's – now results in marriage in which the hero is incorporated into society. But precisely because Christy must not be incorporated into society Synge moves away from domestic comedy to ironic comedy whose basic theme is always the expulsion of the *pharmakos* or scapegoat from society. Frye comments:

> In ironic comedy we begin to see that art has also a lower limit in actual life. This is the condition of savagery, the world in which comedy consists of inflicting pain on a helpless victim, and tragedy in enduring it. Ironic comedy brings us the figure of the scapegoat ritual and the nightmare dream, the human symbol that concentrates our fears and hates.[9]

The ritual of the scapegoat awakens echoes of Christ as scapegoat and indeed Act III is rich with allusions to the ministry of Christ, and especially to the events of Holy Week. The triumphant procession from the strand to the shebeen – 'They're raising him up' – is a comic allusion to Christ's triumphant entry into Jerusalem on an ass. Christy, at this point in the play, is a hero who has reached the apotheosis of his career. Pegeen 'radiantly' wiping Christy's face with her shawl recalls Veronica who wiped the perspiration from Christ's face as He bore His cross to Calvary. In the climactic love scene Christy declares he will marry Pegeen 'when Good Friday's by'. It is a superbly timed ironic stroke that the entry of Old Mahon after the lovers' betrothal signifies the father 'saving' the son from the heroine. It is his entry too which initiates the expulsion of Christy the scapegoat after a judgement scene where the parallels with Christ are obvious:

> MAHON: Rise up now to retribution, and come on with
> me.
> CROWD: *(jeeringly)*. There's the playboy! There's the lad
> thought he'd rule the roost in Mayo. Slate him now,
> Mister.
> CHRISTY: *(getting up in shy terror)*. What is it drives you
> to torment me here, when I'd ask the thunders of the
> might of God to blast me if I ever did hurt to any
> saving only that one single blow.
> MAHON: *(loudly)*. If you didn't, you're a poor good-
> for-nothing and isn't it by the like of you the sins of
> the whole world are committed?
> CHRISTY: *(raising his hands)*. In the name of the Almighty
> God . . . .

The echoes of the Passion in this exchange are further
amplified by the ensuing action. Like Christ who was
clothed in a purple robe and mocked, Christy is mocked
by being clothed in women's petticoats. He is bound,
tortured and sentenced to die on the gallows tree.

Christy arrives at an understanding of his destiny very
late in the play. When he is first rejected by Pegeen he
recoils in horror from his fate:

> And I must go back into my torment is it, or run off like
> a vagabond straying through the Unions with the dusts
> of August making mudstains in the gullet of my throat,
> or the winds of March blowing on me till I'd take an
> oath I felt them making whistles of my ribs within.

Since he is under the illusion that the only way to regain
Pegeen's love and so avoid such a fate is to kill his father

physically, he attempts to do so. But again he is rejected by Pegeen who points out that 'there's a great gap between a gallous story and a dirty deed.' In the harsh light of reality the mythic story of Christy's parricide has become a lie, the mythic deed a 'squabble in your backyard'. It is, finally, Pegeen's denial of the possibility of bridging story and deed through the imagination, coupled with her torturing Christy, that makes him accept his destiny. 'Cut the rope,' he tells her, 'and I'll quit the lot of you and live from this out like the madmen of Keel, eating muck and green weeds on the faces of the cliffs.' The stage directions indicate that he now even accepts his destiny with a kind of exaltation. He speaks *'almost gaily'*; when he bites Shawn he is *'delighted with himself'*; when Pegeen burns him he screams 'Oh, glory be to God!' as if in triumph that he will finally escape the house he had once called safe. At this point he faces his father again – 'Are you coming to be killed a third time . . . ?' – but the third 'murder', unlike the others, is symbolic and decisive. It does not depend on lies or on violence; Christy triumphs because he is now a free man able to exercise a moral ascendancy over his father. Paradoxically, this symbolic murder reconciles father and son. In *The Shadow of the Glen* the Tramp and Nora depart to seek a better world leaving Dan Burke with Michael Dara; here father and son now set off on the roads leaving Pegeen to keen the loss of a happiness she was afraid to accept.

Christy's last words are a blessing on the villagers who 'in the end of all' have turned him into a man, a 'likely gaffer', 'the way I'll go romancing through a romping lifetime from this day to the dawning of the judgement day'. These final words anticipate the optimism voiced by Stephen Dedalus at the end of *A Portrait of the Artist as a Young Man*: 'Welcome, O life! I go to encounter for the millionth time the reality of experience and to forge in the smithy of my soul the uncreated conscience of my race.' But when we meet Stephen again in *Ulysses* we discover that he has never realized his ambitious dreams, that he is a mere asethete and the butt of Joyce's irony. We do not have a further portrait of the Playboy, but if the irony which had touched the departures of the Tramp and the blind beggars of *The Well of the Saints* be applied here, Christy's fate may resemble more closely that of Don Quixote, the Knight of the Sorrowful Countenance, than that of a playboy romancing his way through a romping lifetime.

It has been the tendency among critics to characterize those Dublin audiences which rioted when *The Playboy of the Western World* was first presented as bigoted and narrow- minded. But to claim that they rioted because of the offence caused by the use of the word 'shift', or to argue, as did Yeats, that the opposition was formed by people who had no books in their homes, is patently untrue. Opponents like Arthur Griffith, Maud Gonne, Padraic Colum and Padraic Pearse were neither puritanical nor ill-read. They represented the Catholic intelligentsia of Ireland, an intelligentsia that was extremely sensitive to the racial stereotyping so long associated with the stage Irishman and to the racist stereotyping that was common in the cartoons of English journals like *Punch*. In reaction, they idealized Ireland and all things Irish and if some disapproved of Yeats's *Countess Cathleen,* they approved enthusiastically of his *Cathleen Ni Houlihan,* which extolled Ireland's beauty and the virtues of patriotism. But *The Playboy* with its glorification of parricide and its portrayal of degeneracy and violence and betrayal seemed – and was – an assault on Nationalist idealism.

That image of the lines of Mayo girls naked under their shifts merely provided the pretext for the protests.

Hostility to *The Playboy* was further increased by the way in which Yeats – with a certain malice – insisted on continuing the play under the protection of the Dublin police, symbol of English colonialism. To add insult to injury, Yeats and Lady Gregory rounded up a claque of students from Trinity College – bastion of pro-English Protestant culture and privilege – who baited the opposition by singing the English national anthem. Yeats always flattered himself that he, unlike Synge, knew the politics of contemporary Ireland; in fact, he understood little of the fierce patriotism that fired men and women like Pearse and Maud Gonne and the others he celebrates so ambiguously in his poem, 'Easter 1916'.

There were some – including Lady Gregory – who were offended by *The Playboy* on aesthetic grounds. George Moore, for example, wrote to Synge about the play's conclusion:

> If what I hear is true, [that] the audience accepted your play gleefully up to the last five minutes of the third act, I confess to sympathizing with the audience. Your play does not end, to my thinking, satisfactorily. Your end is not comedy, it ends on a disagreeable note, and that is always a danger, especially when one chooses parricide as the subject of a jest.[10]

Moore went on to fault the cruelty of the ending. 'The burning of Christy's legs with the coal is quite intolerable and wouldn't be acceptable to any audience – French, German, or Russian.'

Although Moore was later to retract this criticism, it is clear that he was disturbed by Synge's characteristic habit of switching genres so abruptly, and puzzled by his thwarting of expectations established by an earlier aesthetic mode. 'But the element of *play* is the barrier that separates art from savagery,' Northrop Frye writes, 'and playing at human sacrifice seems to be an expected part of ironic comedy.'[11] If we freeze the action of the final scene where Christy is bound on the floor by the drunken villagers and is burned by Pegeen and where he turns, animal-like, to kill his father a third time, the element of play is tenuous, almost lost – as if we had already passed into the Theatre of Cruelty.

Synge was always very sensitive to the charge that he, who so loved the Irish people, had libelled them. After *The Playboy* riots he wrote to a young playwright defending his art:

> In the same way you see – what it seems so impossible to get our Dublin people to see, obvious as it is – that the wildness and, if you will, vices of the Irish peasantry are due, like their extraordinary good points of all kinds, to the *richness* of their nature – a thing that is priceless beyond words.   *(Plays* II,p. xxiii)

This is well said; one is reminded of Byron's dismissal of those who judged his masterpiece, *Don Juan,* to be immoral. 'It may be profligate, but is it not *life,* is it not *the thing?'*

8
'Deirdre of the Sorrows'

The story of Deirdre, of whom it was prophesied that she would bring destruction on the Sons of Usna, is one of the most beautiful and touching of the Irish legends, and has inspired retelling by such writers as Sir Samuel Ferguson, A. E., Eva Gore-Booth, W. B. Yeats and James Stephens.[1] While in Aran, in either 1900 or 1901, Synge made a translation of the Irish text, *The Fate of the Children of Uisneach,* which had been published in 1898 by the Society for the Preservation of the Irish Language. When, in 1902, he reviewed Lady Gregory's *Cuchulain of Muirthemne,* he singled out Deirdre's lament over the dead Naisi and his brothers as 'one of the finest passages in the book'. *(Prose,* p, 369) He wrote to Molly Allgood in 1906, 'My next play must be quite different from the *P. Boy.* I want to do something quiet and stately and restrained and I want you to act in it.'[2] But *The Playboy* and illness prevented him turning to the new play; on 22 October 1907, he wrote to Molly: 'I got a "Deirdre" fit yesterday and I wrote 10 pages of it in great spirits and joy, but alas I know that that is only the go off. There'll be great anguish still before I get her done if I ever do.' His subsequent letters document the degree of his anguish as he strove in his final illness to finish a play with so poignant and personal a theme. It gave him great trouble – he rewrote Act II more than twenty times – and he died before he could complete the play to his satisfaction.

Deirdre of the Sorrows tells the well-known folk tale of a young, beautiful girl, promised as the bride of an elderly king, who elopes with a young man, and of the lovers' subsequent tragic return home. In the play Deirdre and Naisi, one of the Sons of Usna, defy Conchubor, King of Ulster, by wedding and fleeing to Scotland. After seven years Deirdre fears the decay of their love and driven by some tragic necessity returns with Naisi to Ulster where they will die.

The first act of *Deirdre of the Sorrows* is a fine example of economy, invention, dramatic *brio* and proportion. The dominant symbol of the act is storm as the dominant symbol of Act III is the receding tide. Two old women voice their apprehensions about what is to happen and bring the central characters before us: Conchubor on his way from his palace to visit Deirdre, the Sons of Usna hunting in the hills where Deirdre is wandering. The incompatibility between Conchubor and Deirdre, most evident in their age – he is 'about sixty', she a child – emerges in their opening exchange:

> CONCHUBOR: The gods save you, Deirdre. I have come
> up bringing you rings and jewels from Emain Macha.
> DEIRDRE: The gods save you.
> CONCHUBOR: What have you brought from the hills?
> DEIRDRE *(quite self-possessed)*. A bag of nuts, and twigs.

The opposition between society and nature represented by the palace of Emain Macha and the nuts and twigs is continued in the characters of the King and Deirdre. He is old, pathetic, a creature of power and money; Deirdre is young, wilful, a creature of instinct and imagination. 'What we all need is a place is safe and splendid, and it's that you'll get in Emain in two days or three,' the King, obsessed by thoughts of old age, argues. 'I'm well used to the tracks and pathways and the people of the glen,' Deirdre pleads in return. In Act II the lovers will be driven to give up the natural world and return to society where in the apocalyptic finale of Act III Emain is burned and the lovers' illusions about the immortality of their love is exposed.

The finale is adumbrated most dramatically by Synge's use of the storm in Act I. When Deirdre had first met Naisi, before the play opens, she had told him to come to her hut if a storm broke out – if the 'river's rose on the pathways and the floods gathered from the butt of the hills.' Following the departure of King Conchubor, she questions Lavarcham:

DEIRDRE: Are the stepping stones flooding, Lavarcham? Will the night be stormy in the hills?
LAVARCHAM: *(looking at her curiously)*. The stepping stones are flooding surely, and the night will be the worst I'm thinking we've seen these years gone by.

Reference is made again to this ominous night and storm immediately after Naisi has been killed:

DEIRDRE: Do not raise a hand to touch me.
CONCHUBOR: There are other hands to touch you. My fighters are set round in the trees.

J. M. Synge

DEIRDRE: *(almost mockingly).* Who'll fight the grave, Conchubor, and it opened on a dark night?

The night of storm in Act I when the floods gathered 'from the butt of the hills' opened the graves of Act III which are dug 'at the butt of a hill'.

In most versions of the legend of the Sons of Usna Naisi had played the dominant role, Deirdre a subservient one. But Synge, whose plays are dominated by masterful women – Maurya, Nora Burke, Sarah Casey, Molly Byrne, Pegeen Mike – casts Deirdre in the same mould. Both Lavarcham and Old Woman refer continually to Deirdre's wilfulness, wildness and sense of self-esteem. 'Who'd check her like was made to have her pleasure only . . . she without a thought but for her beauty and to be straying the hills,' Lavarcham observes. 'If I was Conchubor I wouldn't marry with her like at all,' Old Woman says and Lavarcham answers resignedly, 'When all's said it's her like will be the master till the ends of time.' 'I'm too long taking my will,' Deirdre warns Conchubor, 'and it's that way I'll be living always.'

She is direct, even brutal, in her seduction of Naisi, balancing the dreadful outcome of their union against the intensity of the present moment. 'Do many know what is foretold, that Deirdre will be the ruin of the Sons of Usna, and have a little grave by herself, and a story will be told forever?' 'It should be a sweet thing to have what is best and richest,' she argues, 'if it's for a short space only.' 'I'm a long while in the woods with my own self,' she tempts Naisi, 'and I'm in little dread of death, and it earned with richness would make the sun red with envy.' *(Plays* II, pp. 209–11) It is a powerful Irish restatement of the *carpe diem* theme to make the most of time:

140

Persuaded by Deirdre's argument, Naisi capitulates and offers her a 'safe place' in communion with the world of nature:

> The stars are out Deirdre, and let you come with me quickly, for it is the stars will be our lamps many nights and we abroad in Alban, and taking our journeys among the little islands in the sea. There has never been the like of the joy we'll have Deirdre, you and I having our fill of love at the evening and the morning till the sun is high.

The act closes beautifully and theatrically with the wedding of Deirdre and Naisi; in its evocation of love and death the scene is reminiscent of the close of Keats's 'The Eve of St Agnes', where the lovers escape into the stormy night.

If Act I is dramatically one of the best things Synge put his hand to, Act II is probably the weakest. In the MacCurtin text, *Oidhe Chloinne Uisnigh,* which he translated, it is Naisi's homesickness and his belief that Conchubor will honour his word not to harm them which causes him to return – Deirdre has no say in the matter. But in Synge's version it is Deirdre who decides to return and for reasons which are too psychological and interiorized – though consistent with the key motifs of his previous plays – to give dramatic momentum and life to the act. Deirdre's reasons, echoed by Naisi, are characteristically Synge's. They will return to Ireland because they fear the horror of ageing, the loss of physical beauty, and the consequent decay of love. Says Deirdre:

> I've dread going or staying, Lavarcham. It's lonesome

this place having happiness like ours till I'm asking each day, will this day match yesterday, and will tomorrow take a good place beside the same day in the year that's gone, and wondering all times is it a game worth playing, living on until you're dried and old, and our joy is gone forever. (*Plays* II, p. 219)

This is well said but, unfortunately, the same sentiment is repeated again and again in Act II by Deirdre and Naisi and Owen; the act attempts to dramatize a truism about the passing of youth and love but ends by being expository and tendentious. What Synge fails to do here he did effectively, and with economy, in *The Playboy of the Western World* where similar sentiments on loneliness, ageing and love are developed in a number of exchanges between Christy and Pegeen and Christy and the Widow Quin. Synge was well aware of the danger of writing narrative rather than drama. As late as August 1908 he wrote to Molly, 'I've decided to cut off the second act – you remember Jesus Christ says if the second act offend thee pluck it out.'

Synge was unable to make real the lovers' seven idyllic years in Alban. The portrayal of a mature sexual relationship seems outside his range: 'There is no such thing as an ordinarily happy married life in Synge. . . . The only form of change in love which Deirdre can conceive is decay.'[3] This can easily be illustrated from the other plays. It is useful to compare Synge and Keats in this respect. In a poem such as 'Ode to a Nightingale' Keats despairs of the 'real' world where 'Beauty cannot keep her lustrous eyes, / Or new love pine at them beyond tomorrow,' but in the 'Ode on a Grecian Urn' he expresses his doubts about the healthiness of seeking to freeze human love and passion in an unravished Arcady. In *Deirdre of the*

Sorrows Lavarcham does, at one point, state that 'there's little hurt getting old', but the burden of Synge's plays is a profound regret at the swift passage of time and an almost obsessive concern with its ravages.

The introduction of Owen, Conchubor's spy, in Act II represents an attempt on Synge's part to make the play more dramatic. He felt it needed 'a grotesque element mixed into its lyrical melancholy', Yeats observed in his preface to the play, 'to give contrast and to create an impression of solidity'. Like the Fool in *King Lear* Owen dispenses a gnomic wisdom and provides a foil (the 'gross note') to the noble-born protagonists. But Owen was never fully developed and he fails to ground the act in reality; he is a cardboard figure who merely apes the truisms of Deirdre and Naisi – 'Queens get old Deirdre, with their white and long arms going from them.' His love for Deirdre and his death are melodramatic and factitious.

There are some effective scenes in Act II, particularly that where Naisi seeks to persuade Deirdre not to return to Emain Macha even though it is clear she will do so. To his urgent, triple 'Come away' she responds in speeches that are genuinely moving and dramatically effective. 'There's no safe place, Naisi, on the ridge of the world'; 'there is no way to keep life and love with it a short space only'; 'there's nothing lonesome like a love is watching out the time most lovers do be sleeping.' Her final speech of farewell to youth and life sets the key for the superb final act:

Woods of Cuan, woods of Cuan . . . . It's seven years we've had a life was joy only and this day we're going west, this day we're facing death maybe and *(goes and looks toward Owen)* death should be a poor untidy thing, though it's a queen that dies.

The open grave on stage in the third act is most fitting. Like the bundle of clothes in *Riders to the Sea,* the grave reinforces the play's intensity and adds a degree of suspense to the inevitability of the action. It is also used to bring about a surprising *rapprochement.* As the quarrel between Conchubor and Naisi progresses by the edge of the grave, Synge intensifies further the tragic character of the catastrophe by having Deirdre effect a reconciliation among lover, loved one and rival. The grave, she argues, is the ultimate reality which renders human emotions – love and hate – irrelevant:

> DEIRDRE: I'll say so near that grave we seem three lonesome people, and by a new made grave there's no man will keep brooding on a woman's lips, or on the man he hates.

This reversal, which seems to offer escape, is followed by another even more powerful and harrowing reversal when Deirdre and Naisi quarrel by the grave immediately before Naisi's death. It is an astringently characteristic touch paralleling Maurya's refusal in *Riders to the Sea* to bless Bartley before he too goes to his death. 'And you'll have me meet death with a hard word from your lips in my ears?' Naisi cries out, aghast. Deirdre, in brutal language, goes on to denounce their seven years in Alban as 'a dream' and demands his death. This final quarrel, where Yeats felt the lovers lose all they had given their life to keep, has its parallels also in the scene where Martin curses Molly in *The Well of the Saints* and in the scene in *The Playboy* where Pegeen betrays and tortures Christy.

It was Synge's intention to make Act III of *Deirdre of the Sorrows* 'Rider-like' and there are obvious similarities. The final scene where Deirdre mourns the death of the

Sons of Usna resembles Maurya's lament for the loss of her sons; both threnodies are delivered to the accompaniment of the *caoine*. There are a number of similarities too in the development of the threnodies. In speech after speech Deirdre moves from self-pity ('who'll pity Deirdre?') through affirmation ('It's you three will not see age or death coming'), elegiac remembrance ('It was the voice of Naisi that was strong in summer'), words of burial ('Let us throw down clay on my three comrades'), resolve to die ('I will not leave Naisi'), prophetic utterance ('because of me . . . there will be a story told of a ruined city and a raving king and a woman will be young forever'). The final note is tragic exaltation:

> I have put sorrow away like a shoe that is worn and muddy, for it is I have had a life that will be envied by great companies. It was not by a low birth I made kings uneasy, and they sitting in the halls of Emain. It was not a low thing to be chosen by Conchubor, who was wise, and Naisi had no match for bravery . . . . It is not a small thing to be rid of grey hairs and the loosening of the teeth. *(With a sort of triumph)*. . . . It was the choice of lives we had in the clear woods, and in the grave we're safe surely.

It is a magnificent closing speech – astonishingly crammed with details of the actress's business – but it should not distract us from the fact that the lovers, for all their heroic passions, have been defeated by life. Synge's austere and tragic view of life first dramatized in *Riders to the Sea* is reaffirmed in our final glimpse of King Conchubor broken, like King Oedipus or King Lear, by the slaughter of those near to him through kinship or desire:

LAVARCHAM: I have a little hut where you can rest Conchubor, there is a great dew falling.

CONCHUBOR: *(with the voice of an old man)*. Take me with you, I'm hard set to see the way before me.

It is difficult to resist the conclusion that in his last play Synge glorifies a death-wish. The dominant *leitmotif* of the play is a horror of life which brings ageing and which entails (for Deirdre) an inevitable loss of beauty and a consequent blighting of love. The motif of the first scene between Deirdre and Naisi was 'welcome to destruction', and Synge characterizes the scene where Deirdre commits suicide as 'defiance of life'. The quarrel scene with Naisi parallels the scene in *Riders to the Sea* where Maurya refuses Bartley her blessing; both women send their men to their deaths because, for different reasons, they perceive death to be good. Life, in Synge's final play, is often described in images of decay while death is usually praised. Naisi's death 'will have no match'; 'It's you [the sons of Usna] will not see age or death coming'; 'it was a clean death was your share, Naisi'; 'Draw back a little from Naisi who is young forever'; 'a woman will be young forever'; 'it is not a small thing to be rid of grey hairs and the loosening of the teeth'; 'in the grave we're safe surely.' In Act I Conchubor had offered Deirdre Emain Macha as 'a place is safe and splendid'; in Act II Naisi had offered her a refuge in nature – 'Come away into the safety of the woods'; but in Act III Deirdre comes finally to realize that only in the grave is she safe, just as Maurya was brought to the same bitter realization: 'Bartley will have a fine coffin out of the white boards, and a deep grave surely . . . . What more can we want than that?'

There is, further, a striking resemblance between Synge's *Deirdre of the Sorrows* and Wagner's *Tristan and*

Isolde which he undoubtedly knew from his musical studies. Both works memorialize the doomed lovers of two famous Celtic legends; both express the anguish of a personal hopeless love (Synge's for Molly Allgood, Wagner's for Mathilde von Wesendonck); both celebrate the theme of Love-as-Death *(Liebestod)* which brings the lovers an ultimate freedom and an eternal youth. To Naisi's statement that the grave puts 'a great space between two friends that love', Deirdre counters, 'maybe it's that grave when it's closed will make us one forever.'

It might seem, on first glance, that the epic story of Deirdre's tragic love for Naisi lay outside the scope and character of Synge's dramatic genius. *The Well of the Saints* and *The Playboy of the Western World* seem the very antithesis of an art that is 'quiet and stately and restrained'. In his poem, 'The Passing of the Shee', he had derided A. E.'s mystical attraction to heroic Celtic figures like 'sweet Angus, Maeve and Fand', choosing instead the tough peasant note:

> We'll search in Red Dan Sally's ditch,
> And drink in Tubber fair,
> Or poach with Red Dan Philly's bitch
> The badger and the hare.   (*Poems,* p. 38)

An earlier version of this poem had a couplet which curtly dismissed A. E. as 'Rhyming reems of bloody rot'.

But if Synge dismisses A. E. so cavalierly it is because he felt that his art lacked a 'grip on reality'. In a series of notes written in 1908, Synge tried to solve the problems inherent in writing on historical or saga stories. He felt that with a very few exceptions historical plays and novels and poems ('Utopian work') were 'relatively worthless'.

But there were methods by which one might avoid 'artificial retellings of classical or saga stories'. The first was to recognize that the place of religious art had been taken by 'our quite modern feeling for the beauty and mystery of nature . . . . Our pilgrimages are not to Canterbury or Jerusalem, but to Killarney and Cumberland and the Alps.' *(Prose,* p. 351) *Deirdre of the Sorrows* surpasses any of Synge's plays in its evocation of 'the beauty and mystery' of Nature. Speech after speech is crammed with descriptions of nature which operate dramatically rather than merely poetically. Naisi's dread and relief after he has discussed his fear of seeing Deirdre grow old are vividly dramatized in images drawn from nature:

> I've had dread, I tell you, dread winter and summer, and the autumn and the spring-time, even when there's a bird in every bush making his own stir till the fall of night. But this talk's brought me ease, and I see we're as happy as the leaves on the young trees and we'll be so ever and always though we'd live the age of the eagle and the salmon and the crow of Britain.

Deirdre, who has overheard Naisi's admission, poses the tragedy of their departure and death against poignant memories of their love amid the woods of Cuan:

> There's no place to stay always . . . . It's a long time we've had, pressing the lips together, going up and down, resting in our arms, Naisi, waking with the smell of June in the top of the grasses, and listening to the birds in the branches that are highest . . . . It's a long time we've had, but the end has come surely.

When Ainnle weds the lovers it is in language drawn not

from theology but from nature: 'By the sun and moon and the whole earth, I wed Deirdre to Naisi. . . . May the air bless you, and water and the wind, the sea, and all the hours of the sun and moon.' It was through the immediacy of such observations based on nature that Synge hoped to make his saga theme more real.

A second method was to demythologize his characters and forge for them a speech which would further humanize them. Synge's King Conchubor is less a king than an ageing father–lover. In Act I he enters accompanied only by Fergus, and his two scenes with Lavarcham and Deirdre portray him as a rather pathetic figure, stiff in the company of the servant, suppliant in his attitude to Deirdre. Deirdre, too, is first presented like any peasant girl – '*poorly dressed with a little bag and a bundle of twigs in her arms*'. With the exception of the scene in Act I where Deirdre dresses herself in the robes of a queen, she is presented as a child–woman doomed to a tragic fate rather than as a queen. The same process of demythologizing extends to Naisi who behaves less like a prince than a hunter and lover associated, like Deirdre, with the natural world. The many drafts of *Deirdre of the Sorrows* show Synge constantly seeking to re-create the remote world of Cuchulain and the Red Branch within the tragic and human dimensions of lover, loved one and rival.

The question of language was also uppermost in Synge's mind as he worked on the play. 'These saga people, when one comes to deal with them, seem very remote,' he wrote to John Quinn on 4 January 1908; 'one does not know what they thought or what they are or where they went to sleep, so one is apt to fall into rhetoric.' *(Plays* II,p. xxvi) In a 1905 review of A.H. Leahy's *Heroic Romances of Ireland,* volume I, Synge terms Leahy's translation of the Deirdre legend a 'deplorable misrepresentation of the spirit of these old verses' done in a 'tawdry commonplace jingle'. *(Prose,* p. 372) Lady Gregory's translations of the Cuchulain cycle he had praised because of the way she combined an Elizabethan vocabulary – 'the only form of English that is quite suitable for incidents of the epic kind' *(Prose,*p. 368) – with the Gaelic constructions of the peasant class. Synge had used such a language in *The Playboy,* but evidently he felt he needed a less colourful style for *Deirdre of the Sorrows,* something closer in rhythm and vocabulary to that of *Riders to the Sea.* The new style had to be more versatile in order to accommodate both the vigour and the colloquialism of peasant speech and the wider emotional range and intensity of the noble-born key characters.

With this in mind Synge in 1907 and 1908 conducted a number of experiments in translating poems by Villon, Muset, Leopardi and Petrarch into prose. A translation of a poem by Villon illustrates how Synge 'Irished' his French model:

That's what's left over from the beauty of a right woman – a bag of bones, and legs the like of two shrivelled sausages going beneath it. It's of the like of that we old hags do be thinking, of the good times are gone away from us, and we crouching on our hunkers by a little fire of twigs, soon kindled and soon spent, we that were the pick of many.   *(Poems,* p. 80)

Synge strikes a slightly more rhetorical style in his translations from Petrarch's sonnet sequence 'Laura in Death':

Life is flying from me, not stopping an hour, and Death is making great strides following my track. The days about me, and the days passed over me are bringing me desolation, and the days to come will be the same surely. *(Poems,* p. 86)

It is significant that Synge translates from poetry into prose as if he felt that his earlier experiments in verse drama – the fragmentary *A Vernal Play, Luasnad, Capa and Laine,* and *The Lady O'Connor* – had led him to write in the idiom of closet drama, like that used by A. E. in his *Deirdre.* Synge's prose is poetic, but the poetry justifies itself dramatically;

> I was in the woods at the full moon and I heard a voice singing. Then I gathered up my skirts, and I ran on a little path I have to the verge of a rock, and I saw you pass by underneath, in your crimson cloak, singing a song, and you standing out beyond your brothers are called the flower of Ireland. *(Plays* II, p. 209)

It is a versatile style which permits the intensity Synge aspires to in the tragic finale:

> I see the flames of Emain starting upward in the dark night, and because of me there will be weasels and wild cats crying on a lonely wall where there were queens and armies, and red gold, the way there will be a story told of a ruined city and a raving king and a woman will be young forever. *(Plays* II, p. 267)

Synge died before he could complete the final work. And yet there are great unfinished works of art – Keats's *The Fall of Hyperion,* Shelley's *The Triumph of Life,* Schubert's Eighth Symphony – which somehow transcend the limitation of their incompleteness. It may be that the earlier works of an artist help in suggesting how the final work would have been completed, as the broken columns of a Greek temple invite us to reconstruct in our imagination the masterpiece that was. *Deirdre of the Sorrows* is a recapitulation on a grand scale of themes, motifs and dramatic methods which characterize Synge's entire *oeuvre*. Always at the centre of his drama there is the struggle between those forces that restrict human liberty and those energies that seek to enhance it. Most commonly Synge, reflecting perhaps his own reaction to the repressive religious creed in which he was raised, opposes the peasant and the tinker to the institutionalized ethic of the Church. On a more metaphysical level he celebrates the richness of the individual who lives out his tragicomic existence within a nihilistic universe that offers neither meaning nor hope. There is in all his work a profound sense of mortality linked to a pathetic reaching out by all his characters for a finer destiny which always seems to be denied them. There are striking affinities between Nora and Deirdre, as there are striking affinities among the Tramp and Martin Doul and Christy Mahon. They represent the imaginative side of life as opposed to the materialism of those they reject – Dan Burke, the Saint, the Priest, Conchubor and even Pegeen Mike.

In his early essay, 'On a Train to Paris', Synge had been deeply moved by the young ballet dancers whom he had saluted as gladiators fated to die in the arena of life. But he had also been struck by their high spirits, good humour and obscenity. It was Synge's originality to have incorporated into his tragic view of life these very qualities, thus giving his work a forceful dramatic astringency. His lonely tramps and beggars at the Irish crossroads are curiously contemporary in their obscenity and fantasies and games; there is a metatheatricality about them as they create and re-create themselves in ever-new roles. To say that Synge's work is contemporary is to recognize that while his plays are a priceless portion of the Irish dramatic movement, they belong also to the wider *patria* of twentieth-century drama.

References

1. A Brief Life

1. Quoted in David H. Greene and Edward M. Stephens, *J. M. Synge 1871–1909* (New York: Macmillan, 1959) pp. 4, 75. Biographical details of Synge's life and family are drawn from this source unless otherwise indicated.

2. W. B. Yeats, *Autobiographies* (London: Macmillan, 1955) pp. 115–16.

3. Yeats (ed.), *Beltaine,* no. 2 (London: Cass, 1970) pp. 7, 12.

4. W. I. Thompson, *The Imagination of an Insurrection* (New York: Oxford University Press, 1967) p. 238.

5. Yeats, *Essays and Introductions* (London: Macmillan, 1961) pp. 209–10.

6. H. Gorman, *James Joyce* (London: The Bodley Head, 1949) pp. 101, 254.

7. Quoted in Greene and Stephens, p. 173.

8. Yeats, *Autobiographies,* pp. 563–4.

9. A. Saddlemyer (ed.), *Letters to Molly* (Cambridge, Mass.: Harvard University Press, 1971) p. xxi.

10. Yeats, *Explorations* (London: Macmillan, 1962) p. 226.

11. See Ulick O'Connor, *Oliver St John Gogarty* (London:

Jonathan Cape, 1964) p. 123.

   12.   Yeats, *Autobiographies,* p. 507.
   13.   Yeats, *Essays and Introductions,* p. 306.

2.   A Passage to the Aran Islands

   1.   R. Skelton, *The Writings of J. M. Synge* (London: Thames & Hudson, 1971) p. 62.
   2.   M. Bourgeois, *John M. Synge and the Irish Theatre* (New York: Blom, 1965) p. 92.
   3.   'Civilization is falling from me little by little. . . . I have escaped everything that is artificial, conventional, customary. I am entering into the truth, into nature.' Paul Gauguin, *Noa Noa,* trans. O. F. Theis (New York: Farrar, Strauss & Co., 1957) pp. 40–41.
   4.   N. Grene, *Synge: A Critical Study of the Plays* (London: Macmillan, 1975) p. 32.
   5.   T. S. Eliot, *Selected Essays,* ed. J. Hayward (London: Penguin, 1953) p. 74.
   6.   Grene, p. 78.
   7.   J. Joyce, *Letters,* vol. II, ed. Richard Ellmann (London: Faber & Faber, 1966) p. 212.
   8.   Joyce, 'The Dead', in R. Scholes and A. Walton Litz (eds), *Dubliners* (New York: Viking, 1969) p. 189.
   9.   Yeats, 'In Memory of Major Gregory', *Collected Poems* (London: Macmillan, 1955) p. 149.

3.   Synge and The Theatre

   1.   Yeats, *Autobiographies* p. 381.
   2.   Lady Gregory, *Our Irish Theatre* (London: Putnam, 1913) pp. 8–9.
   3.   Quoted in Greene and Stephens, p. 88.
   4.   Yeats, *The Letters of W. B. Yeats,* ed. Allan Wade (London: Macmillan, 1954) p. 310.
   5.   Yeats, *Explorations,* pp. 107–9.
   6.   Ibid., p. 74.
   7.   Ibid., p. 96.

8. Yeats, *Essays and Introductions* p. 322.
9. Yeats, 'The Municipal Gallery Revisited', *Collected Poems,* p. 369.
10. Yeats (ed.), *Beltaine,* no. 1, p. 8.
11. Yeats, *Essays and Introductions,* p. 221.
12. Quoted in Greene and Stephens, p. 229.
13. Yeats, *Explorations,* p. 250.
14. F. J. Fay, *Towards a National Theatre,* ed. R. Hogan (Dublin: Dolmen, 1970) p. 54.
15. Yeats, quoted in Dawson Byrne, *The Story of Ireland's National Theatre* (New York: Haskell, 1971) p. 25.
16. Fay, p. 16.
17. Bourgeois, pp. 129–31.
18. In *The Critical Writings of James Joyce,* ed. E. Mason and R. Ellmann (London: Faber & Faber, 1959) p. 70.
19. Yeats, *Explorations,* p. 86.
20. Marie Nic Shiubhlaigh and Edward Kenny, *The Splendid Years* (Dublin: Duffy, 1955) p. 60.
21. W. G. Fay and C. Carswell, *The Fays of the Abbey Theatre* (New York: Harcourt, Brace, 1935) pp. 133–4.
22. Ibid., pp. 138–9.
23. Nic Shiubhlaigh, p. 43.
24. Sean McCann, 'The Theatre Itself', in S. McCann (ed.), *The Story of the Abbey Theatre* (London: Four Square Books. 1967) pp. 53–68. See also Dawson Byrne, p. 46.
25. P. P. Howe, *J. M. Synge* (London: Secker, 1912) p. 27.

4. Riders to the Sea

1. D. Johnston, *John Millington Synge* (New York: Columbia University Press, 1965) p. 22.
2. Bourgeois, p. 166.
3. N. Frye, *Anatomy of Criticism* (New Jersey: Princeton University Press, 1957) p. 42.
4. G. Murray, *Euripides and His Age* (New York: Holt, 1913) p. 61.
5. D. Donoghue, 'Synge: "Riders to the Sea": A Study', *University Review,* I (Summer, 1955) 57.
6. Quoted in Grene, p. 55.

References

7.   M. Eliade, *Cosmos and History* (New York: Harper Torchbooks, 1959) p. 96.

8.   Frye, p. 95.

9.   This was first noted by D. Gerstenberger, *John Millington Synge* (New York: Twayne, 1964) p. 46.

10.   R. Graves, *The Greek Myths,* vol. I (Harmondsworth: Penguin Books, 1955) p. 48.

11.   Nic Shiubhlaigh p. 55.

12.   E. M Forster, *A Passage to India* (London: Edward Arnold, 1961) p. 156.

13.   Frye, p. 213.

14.   Yeats, 'Blood and the Moon', *Collected Poems,* p. 268.

5.   The Wicklow Plays

1.   V. Mercier, *The Irish Comic Tradition* (Oxford: Clarendon, 1962) p. 239.

2.   Yeats, *Essays and Introductions,* p. 300.

3.   Greene and Stephens, p. 153.

4.   C. E. Montague, *Dramatic Values* (London: Methuen, 1911) p. 54.

5.   Quoted in Greene and Stephens, p. 156.

6.   J. Keats, *The Selected Letters of John Keats,* ed. Lionel Trilling (New York: Farrar, Strauss & Young, 1951) p. 88.

7.   R. Cohn, *Currents in Contemporary Drama* (Bloomington: Indiana University Press, 1971) pp. 155–6.

6.   The Well of the Saints

1.   Fay and Carswell, pp. 167–8.

2.   Quoted in Greene and Stephens, p. 282.

3.   Quoted in Cohn, pp. 55–6.

4.   Quoted in Grene, p. 127.

5.   P. B. Shelley, *Defence of Poetry.*

6.   D. Corkery, *Synge and Anglo-Irish Literature* (Cork: Mercier Paperback, 1966) p. 175.

7.   Quoted in Eric Bentley (ed.), *Naked Masks: Five Plays of Pirandello* (New York: Dutton, 1957) p. xiv.

J. M. Synge

7. The Playboy of the Western World

1. Bourgeois, p. 203.
2. J. F. Kilroy, 'The Playboy as Poet', PMLA, LXXXIII (1968) 439–42; Mary R. Sullivan, 'Synge, Sophocles and the Un-Making of Myth', *Modern Drama,* XII (1969) 242–53; S. Sultan, 'A Joycean Look at The Playboy of the Western World', in M. Harmon (ed.), in *The Celtic Master* (Dublin: Dolmen Press, 1969) pp. 44–55; R. R. Sanderlin, 'Synge's *Playboy* and the Ironic Hero', *The Southern Quarterly,* VI (1968) 289–301; T. R. Whitaker (ed.), 'Introduction: On Playing with *The Playboy*', in *Twentieth Century Interpretations of The Playboy of the Western World* (New Jersey: Prentice-Hall, 1969) pp. 1–20.
3. Nic Shiubhlaigh, p. 81.
4. Mercier, p. 146.
5. Frye, pp. 180–1.
6. Sultan, pp. 44–55.
7. Greene and Stephens, p. 265. In the same letter Synge qualifies what he calls his 'Extravaganza theory' with the remark, 'Of course *Playboy* is serious.'
8. A. Price, *Synge and Anglo-Irish Drama* (London: Methuen, 1961) p. 170.
9. Frye, p. 45.
10. Greene and Stephens, p. 255.
11. Frye, p. 46.

8. Deirdre of the Sorrows

1. For a detailed study of the Deirdre legend, see H. V. Fackler, *That Tragic Queen: The Deirdre Legend in Anglo-Irish Literature* (Salzburg: Universität Salzburg, 1978).
2. Saddlemyer, p. 67.
3. Grene, p. 177.

Bibliography

(i) Primary Sources

Saddlemyer, Ann (ed.), *Letters to Molly: John Millington Synge to Maire O'Neill 1906–1909* (Cambridge, Mass.: Harvard University Press, 1971).
Skelton, Robin (gen. ed.), *J. M. Synge: Collected Works* (Oxford University Press, 1962–8).
  Volume I: *Poems,* ed. Robin Skelton, 1962.
  Volume II: *Prose,* ed. Alan Price, 1966.
  Volumes III and IV: *Plays,* ed. Ann Saddlemyer, 1968.

(ii) Secondary Sources

Bourgeois, Maurice, *John Millington Synge and the Irish Theatre* (New York: Blom, 1965).
Clark, David R. (ed.), *Riders to the Sea* (Ohio: Merrill Literary Casebook Series, 1970).
Corkery, Daniel, *Synge and Anglo-Irish Literature* (Cork: Mercier Paperback, 1966).
Gerstenberger, Donna, *John Millington Synge* (New York: Twayne, 1964).

J. M. Synge

Greene, D. H. and Stephens, E. M., *J. M. Synge 1871–1909* (New York: Macmillan, 1959).

Grene, Nicholas, *Synge: A Critical Study of the Plays* (London: Macmillan, 1975).

Kiberd, Declan, *Synge and the Irish Language* (New Jersey: Rowman & Littlefield, 1979).

Levitt, Paul M., *J. M. Synge: A Bibliography of Published Criticism* (New York: Barnes & Noble, 1974).

Price, Alan, *Synge and Anglo-Irish Drama* (London: Methuen, 1961).

Saddlemyer, Ann, *Synge and Modern Comedy* (Dublin: Dolmen, 1968).

Skelton, Robin, *The Writings of J. M. Synge* (London: Thames & Hudson, 1971).

Whitaker, T. R. (ed.), *Twentieth Century Interpretations of the Playboy of the Western World* (New Jersey: Prentice-Hall, 1969).

Yeats, W.B., *Essays and Introductions* (London: Macmillan, 1961).

_____, *Explorations* (London: Macmillan, 1962).

Index

Index

Index

Index

Index